Nurture Groups in Schools

Education at SAGE

SAGE is a leading international publisher of journals, books, and electronic media for academic, educational, and professional markets.

Our education publishing includes:

- accessible and comprehensive texts for aspiring education professionals and practitioners looking to further their careers through continuing professional development

- inspirational advice and guidance for the classroom

- authoritative state of the art reference from the leading authors in the field

Find out more at: **www.sagepub.co.uk/education**

Nurture Groups in Schools

Principles and Practice
Second Edition

Marjorie Boxall
Revised and updated by Sylvia Lucas

Los Angeles | London | New Delhi
Singapore | Washington DC

First edition published 2002
Reprinted 2002, 2004, 2005, 2006, 2007, 2008

SAGE Publications Ltd
1 Oliver's Yard
55 City Road
London EC1Y 1SP

SAGE Publications Inc.
2455 Teller Road
Thousand Oaks, California 91320

SAGE Publications India Pvt Ltd
B 1/I 1 Mohan Cooperative Industrial Area
Mathura Road
New Delhi 110 044

SAGE Publications Asia-Pacific Pte Ltd
3 Church Square
10-04 Samsung Hub
Singapore 049483

Library of Congress Control Number: 2009939710

British Library Cataloguing in Publication data

A catalogue record for this book is available from the British Library

ISBN 978-1-84920-418-7
ISBN 978-1-84920-419-4 (pbk)

Typeset by Dorwyn, Wells, Somerset
Printed and bound by CPI Group (UK) Ltd, Croydon, CR0 4YY
Printed on paper from sustainable resources

To the memory of Marjorie Boxall
who gave us permission to be ourselves

Contents

Preface to the Second Edition

When nurture groups were introduced in the Inner London
Education Authority (ILEA), they were ahead of their time. They
were based on inclusive principles at a stage when rolls in
schools for maladjusted pupils were rising rapidly. The concept
offered an explicitly educational response to a set of problems
that were often seen exclusively in terms of psychiatric or
sociological constructs. It was a cost-effective initiative during a
period when expenditure constraints in education were not as
restrictive as they are now. It trained qualified teachers and
unqualified classroom assistants together to create classroom
teams long before the need for such training was generally
recognized.

The abolition of the Inner London Education Authority
almost brought the Nurture Group project to an end. But the
perseverance of a number of primary schools and the strong
support of a handful of other local education authorities
sustained the project through very difficult times. When the
first edition of this book was published, it looked like an
approach whose time had come – inclusive, targeted, systematic and intellectually coherent, with a well-defined curriculum and a clear programme for parental involvement. The
appearance of the first comprehensive handbook on nurture
groups was therefore timely. The decade since the writing of
that first edition has seen a continued expansion in the
number of nurture groups, a growth in the strength of the network that links them and a steady increase in published
research on their efficacy. The problems that Marjorie Boxall
observed in an earlier generation of school children are no less
prevalent now. The strategy she developed for responding to
their needs was a foundation on which many others have been
able to build. Sylvia Lucas has reflected that continuing developmental work in this expanded and updated second edition of
the handbook. So this publication continues to challenge us to

respond to the children's needs with the commitment and clarity of vision that Boxall's original approach expressed.

Tony Cline
Educational Psychology Group, University College London
November 2009

History

Nurture groups had their origin in the 1960s in an area of East London that was in a state of massive social upheaval. Families had been resettled there following slum clearance, migrants from other parts of the UK had moved in, and there was a large recently arrived multicultural immigrant population. The schools were overcrowded and under enormous stress. Children were being excluded from school within weeks of arrival and unprecedented numbers were referred for psychiatric help, virtually all described as violent, aggressive and disruptive. The child guidance clinics modified their work in an attempt to engage with the problems, but the origin and nature of the children's difficulties were outside the conceptual basis of their work.

The children's difficulties seemed related to stress on their parents, historical or personal in origin. This had impaired the nurturing/learning process of the earliest years, and at the time of school entry there was a serious mismatch of child and school. 'The mother is the child's first teacher'; in normal circumstances, her intimate involvement with the child provides his or her first learning experiences and is the model for the work of the nurture group.

The aim of nurture work is to provide a restorative experience of early nurture in the children's neighbourhood school. Two experimental nurture groups were set up in 1970, in an infant and a junior school. They were successful and subsequently spread throughout the ILEA. The Department of Education and Science (DES) watched with interest, delegated Her Majesty's Inspector (HMI), John Woodend, to liaise with the work, and subsequently funded statistical work on the Diagnostic Developmental Profile, now the Boxall Profile (Bennathan and Boxall, 1998). In 1974, the ILEA internally circulated a pamphlet 'The Nurture Group in the Primary School' (essentially Chapter 2 of Bennathan and Boxall, 1996), and more groups followed.

The first edition of this book was based on the collated experience from 1970 to 1989 of more than 50 groups in the ILEA, supplemented by information in relation to practice in Enfield, where all the groups were in infant schools, and established in strictly defined circumstances.

This revised edition takes into account recent developments which have seen over 1000 nurture groups established in secondary schools and special SEBD (social, emotional and behavioural difficulties) schools as well as primary schools across the UK and internationally.

Nurture groups are inclusive provision in mainstream schools for children vulnerable to SEBD and meet the aims of the Every Child Matters agenda. For further information about the Boxall Profile and other available literature, please see www.nurturegroups.org

Acknowledgements

It has been a privilege and a labour of love to be able to revise and update this book. I am indebted to Gill Buckland, Early Years Social Inclusion Co-ordinator for London Borough of Enfield, for her enthusiasm and helpful advice from her LA experience and also to Kim Insley, programme director of the Advanced Educational Practice programme at the Institute of Education, University of London, for a higher education perspective.

Both contributed to the 4 day course: Understanding the Theory and Practice of Nurture Groups, during the time when I was the course leader. Kim now leads the course which is a popular module for PGCE graduates, as is the more recent 'sister' module, Managing the Teaching and Learning in the Nurture Group.

Part 1

INTRODUCTION TO NURTURE GROUPS

1

Overview

This chapter describes:

- what a nurture group is
- how nurture groups help children and young people to succeed in school
- the criteria for a classic nurture group and some variants.

Nurture groups are an inclusive (Howes et al., 2002), educational, in-school resource for mainly primary school children, although increasingly aspects of the nurture approach are being used with some success in both the early years and secondary phases (Bennathan and Rose, 2008). They are for children whose emotional, social, behavioural and cognitive learning needs cannot be met in the mainstream class and who will be or should be at School Action Plus on the SEN register. Their difficulties are markedly varied, often severe, are a cause of underachievement and sometimes lead to exclusion from school. They are rarely considered appropriate for psychotherapy and are usually referred on to a resource within education such as a Pupil Referral Unit (PRU). Typically, such children have grown up in circumstances of stress and adversity sufficiently severe to limit or disturb the nurturing process of the earliest years. To varying extents, they are without the basic and essential learning that normally from birth is bound into a close and trusting relationship with an attentive and responsive parent.

School expectations

Teachers expect new entrants to school to be making progress towards meeting the Early Learning Goals (QCA, 1999) and, in their personal, social and emotional development, to:

- feel secure, trust known adults to be kind and helpful, and concerned about their well-being
- be responsive to them, biddable and cooperative
- approach and respond to other children and speak in a familiar group
- have some understanding of immediate cause and effect
- be eager to extend their past experience, and tolerate the frustration and disappointment of not succeeding
- find the school day stimulating but not overwhelming
- be confident to try new activities and initiate ideas.

This has never been the case for all children. Disquiet, which became more evident in the 1960s, continues into the 21st century. As the gap widens and is perceived more generally to be a barrier to learning, there is recognition at government level of the need to intervene. The Steer report on behaviour in schools, *Learning Behaviour: Lessons Learned* (DCSF, 2009a), considers nurture groups to be an important resource for improving children's behaviour. They have a clear rationale underpinned by sound theory but are easily accessible to practitioners and are cost-effective.

Evaluations from some LAs and individual schools demonstrate that nurture groups are proving to be more economically sustainable than other support provided for vulnerable children. One LA, LB Enfield, has identified the following costings (2009) for children in various support programmes (all figures are approximate):

Complex needs placement in an Enfield school for an Enfield child
(middle band C)   £13,000+ per annum
Out-of-borough day school for one child
(band E)   £17,000+ per annum

(Continued)

(Continued)

EBD out-of-borough residential placement for one child (independent school)   £40,000+ per annum

Full-time LSA support per child   £14,000+ per annum
Nurture group provision (for a minimum of 10 children)   £55,000 per annum

Nurture group provision (for one child)   £5,500 per annum

An established, classic nurture group may have up to 30 children passing through each year, i.e. a regular primary class group size which brings the cost down to **£1,833** per child.

The aim of the nurture group is to create the world of earliest childhood in school, and through this build in the basic and essential learning experiences normally gained in the first three years of life, thus enabling the children to participate fully in the mainstream class, typically within a year. The process is modelled on normal development from birth and the content is the essential precursor of the statutory National Curriculum including the Early Years Foundation Stage (EYFS) (DCSF, 2008a).

Children's difficulties: their nature and origin

Children's difficulties in school are often severe, and sometimes seem bizarre. They range from autistic-like behaviour at one extreme, to disruptive behaviour at the other that may involve physical violence and sometimes exclusion from school. Although not always immediately apparent, many of the children have not reached the developmental level of the normal three-year-old, and are in difficulties from the time they enter school. They undermine the teachers' skills and cause enormous stress and despair, and sometimes negativism. They are not usually felt to be suitable for psychotherapy because to varying extents all aspects of their development have been impaired: their experience is limited, poorly organized and has little coherence, their concepts are imperfect and their feelings confused. They are without a sufficiently organized and coherent past experience from which to develop and there is no clear focus for intervention.

The parents, too, are often difficult to engage. Many of them live under extreme and disabling personal stress. If referred to a mental health resource because of their children's difficulties in school, they have the burden of finding their way to an unfamiliar place to face a bewildering discussion and the visit can be counterproductive. Many first appointments are not kept, and if kept are rarely sustained. The aims of Sure Start and the move to children's centres are welcome but have yet to reach the most disadvantaged. For too many families, it all seems of little relevance, particularly when their situation seems beyond repair; feelings are too chaotic to disentangle, or are submerged under anger or depression.

The children's difficulties seem related to the stage in the earliest years when nurturing care was critically impaired. Over the years, changing historical forces have led to a different distribution of the more clearly defined difficulties; those that are more generalized have increased markedly and over a wider social spectrum.

Children referred to nurture groups fall broadly into two groups, and Chapter 10 has detailed descriptions.

Nurture children

These are reception-age children who are functionally below the age of three, or, if older, at least two to three years below their chronological age; they all have considerable social, emotional, behavioural and learning difficulties. These were relatively clearly defined in the 1960s in the area where nurture groups were originally developed, and it is from this experience that the thinking and practice of the nurture groups derive.

Children who need nurturing

These children are also successfully placed in nurture groups but are not *nurture children*. They are emotionally disorganized, but are not without the basic learning of the earliest years. Other forms of provision for children with SEBD may meet some of their needs although they often continue to underachieve. Teachers may respond intuitively to their underlying need for attachment and provide domestic experiences and family-type relationships but these are not necessarily part of the planned intervention.

Multiple and varied difficulties but shared needs

The difficulties of almost all children in nurture groups are multiple, and a disproportionate number, compared with the general school population, have complicating features such as motor coordination and speech and language difficulties, impaired hearing or sight, or ill health.

Importantly, the teacher works with an assistant within this complexity, without needing to understand how these complex and varied difficulties came about. They rarely need to know the nature of the past stress on the children, and attempting to understand the dynamics of the particular family and the children's perception of themselves and their world is neither feasible nor relevant. The children share a history of early developmental impairment and loss; their common need is for restorative learning experiences at an earlier developmental level.

The basis of nurture work: the teacher's primary task

Nurture work is based on the observation that everyone developmentally ahead of young children seems biologically programmed into relating to them in a developmentally appropriate way. This is the intuitive response that the practitioners bring to their work.

Both adults work together in partnership, using their particular expertise to relate intuitively and appropriately to the children's attachment needs, drawing on an understanding of child development, using observational and assessment skills and having detailed curriculum subject knowledge from the Early Years Foundation Stage (EYFS) through to the age-appropriate National Curriculum levels.

The model

The model is the attentive, interactive process of parents and children in the earliest years within a structure commensurate with the physical and physiological development of babies and toddlers. It focuses and expands on the relational features from recognized child development phases such as those provided in the EYFS materials (DCSF, 2008a). The nurture group model is shown below.

Earliest learning: a summary chart

Figure 1. Early Nurture

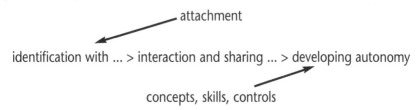

Table 1. The Context of Early Childhood Experiences

Babies/young children in the home	Re-created structures in the nurture group
Babies are emotionally and physically attached from the beginning, are physically dependent and need protection	Close physical proximity in the home area in a domestic setting facilitates emotional and physical attachment.
Experiences are determined by their developmental level (mobility, vision, interest, attention), and parents' intuitive response to their needs.	T/A (teacher and/or assistant) select basic experiences, and control them. They emphasize developmentally relevant features and direct the children's attention to these.
The waking day is short, slow-moving, broken up by rest and routines. There is a clear time structure. Physical needs determine the rhythm of the day.	The day is broken up by slow-moving interludes and routines. Everything is taken slowly, and there is a clear time structure.
Parents provide simple, restricted, repetitive routines and consistent management from the beginning and manageable learning experiences through appropriate play materials and developmentally relevant interaction.	T/A establish routines, emphasize order and routine; ensure much repetition; achieve/convey behavioural expectations by clear prohibitions and limits. Toys and activities are developmentally relevant, and the adults' language and interaction are appropriate for this level.

The situation is made appropriate for an earlier developmental level; it is simpler, more immediate, more routinized, more protected. Restrictions and constraints provide clarity of experience and focus the children's attention; they engage at this level, attention is held and there is much repetition. Basic experiences and attachment to the adults are consolidated. Children experience satisfaction and approval, and attachment to the adults is strengthened. Routine gives security and they anticipate with confidence and pleasure.

Growth-promoting patterns are established.

Table 2. The Content of Early Childhood Experiences

This stage relates to the developmental phase from birth to approximately 11 months.

Attachment and proximity: earliest learning	
Babies/young children in the home	**Re-created structures in the nurture group**
Food, comfort, holding close; consistent care and support.	Food, comfort, close physical contact; consistent care and support.
Cradling, rocking; sensory exploration; touch in communication.	Cradling, rocking; sensory exploration; touch in communication.
Intense concentration on parents' eyes and face. They communicate mood/feelings through face/voice, spontaneously exaggerating their response.	T/A draw children's attention to their eyes and faces, and make and establish eye contact. They deliberately exaggerate their facial expression and tone of voice.
Closeness; intimate interplay; shared feelings/satisfaction. Parents' verbal accompaniment reflects pleasure, and child's loveableness and value. Parents give frequent positive acknowledgement of their child.	There is closeness, intimate interplay and shared feelings/satisfaction. T/A's verbal accompaniment reflects pleasure, and child's loveableness and value. They make frequent positive acknowledgement of each child.
Parents have age-appropriate expectations; accept asocial behaviour but control events and provide manageable constraints and alternatives.	T/A have developmentally appropriate expectations. They tolerate asocial behaviour but give purposeful direction, control events and provide manageable constraints and alternatives.

The foundations of trust, security, positive mood and identity are built in through continuing support and shared basic satisfactions in the context of adult–child emotional attachment and physical proximity. Feelings are communicated and shared, and there is close identification and empathy, the one with the other, and an empathetic response to subtle non-verbal signals. Shared experience, registered in language, leads to an understanding of basic attributes and properties of materials, and of objects and their relationships, and cause and effect.

This stage relates to the developmental phases from approximately 8 to 20 months.

The children have already internalized the security that comes from attachment to reliable, attentive, comforting parents and this security is reinforced through the continuing repetition of the simple routines of daily life. These become a familiar and meaningful sequence of events, and through them children gain a sense that the world is stable, orderly and predictable. In the course of physical maturation in an appropriate environment, basic competencies are acquired. Adequately consistent management of behaviour is experienced, achieved and conveyed by explicit setting of boundaries.

From this secure base, parents help children to personal autonomy through a complex process of letting go and bringing back. They are 'let go' into experiences that the parents control and ensure are manageable, and where support is provided when needed, and they are 'brought back' to the security of close contact with the parents when the situation is overwhelming and they can no longer cope. Because the parents are sensitively involved and intervene when necessary, new experiences are manageable and children are able to assimilate and consolidate them.

Table 3. Letting go and bringing back: developing autonomy

This stage relates to the developmental phases from approximately 16 to 36 months.

Babies/young children in the home	Re-created structures in the nurture group
Children do things with parents, or with parent nearby. There is frequent contact and reassurance and expression of pleasure and approval.	Children do things with T/A, or alongside; are collected together frequently with calmness and reassurance and eye contact is re-established.
Children show spontaneously arising need for transitional objects	T/A make transitional objects available to provide comfort,

(Continued)

(Continued)

providing comfort, support, control.	support, control, and may introduce them.
Parents give attention to simple experiment and repetitive play and of own accord children persist at this level. There is much experiment and repetition.	T/A introduce, demonstrate and share early play, with experiment and repetition. Support and encouragement help them to persist at their developmental level.
Children engage in simple investigation and exploration, and because this is limited by their physical development and parents' intervention, frustration is tolerable.	T/A select basic experiences for investigation and exploration. They control and direct these, anticipate and avoid unmanageable situations and divert attention. Unnecessary frustration is reduced.
Parents give help with basic skills, procedures, and provide information, suggestions, ideas.	T/A give help with basic skills and procedures and provide information, suggestions, ideas.
Parents help/intervene when necessary and often play with children for mutual enjoyment. They share experiences and learn together. Parents respond with pleasure to each new achievement.	T/A help/intervene when necessary and often play with children for mutual enjoyment. They share experiences and learn together. T/A give immediate praise for each small gain.
Relationships are individual. Parents intuitively identify child/object/task by name, and provide a developmentally relevant running commentary.	Requests/instructions to the children are at first individual, never general; child/object/task are specifically named, and there is continuing verbalization.
Children's development is gradual, and simple experiences, in the course of physical maturation, come before complex ones. Parents prepare children for new experiences and anticipate and describe events and feelings in simple language.	Everything is in incremental stages, simple before complex, with the situation structured; essentials highlighted; and complex instructions broken down. There is detailed preparation for each new experience; feelings are anticipated and described.
Sharing and choosing come in manageable stages. There is enough play space. Parents support/control cooperative play with other children; anticipate problems, avert, intervene; identify with and share children's feelings.	The need to share is deliberately limited at first (there is enough for everyone). Grabbing is controlled. Sharing/choosing are built into manageable stages and play space is respected. Cooperative work/play is not expected, but is encouraged,

introduced, controlled. T/A anticipate problems, avert, intervene; identify with and share children's feelings.

Children need/demand order. Parents meet own and children's need for order by providing routine and orderliness. They involve children in orderly routines such as tidying up, sorting out and putting away.

Routines structure the day. Sorting out, tidying up and putting away are stressed. T/A show them what to do.

Parents provide simple, consistent basic training. They make expectations clear and demonstrate. Approval/disapproval is immediate and evident. They give help and reminders when necessary. Verbal commentary and reinforcement at this early level are simple and basic and reflect the achievement.

Simple, consistent, unremitting basic training is provided. T/A make their expectations clear and constantly stress them, with demonstration when appropriate. They give immediate and evident approval/disapproval and help and reminders when necessary. Their verbal commentary and reinforcement reflect children's level and achievement.

The situation is made manageable and support is there when needed; new experiences are assimilated and consolidated, and the children explore with purpose and confidence. They become personally better organized and realize that they have some control over their environment. They learn to give and take and control their own behaviour, and make constructive relationships that provide satisfaction and extend their horizons. They can now manage on their own for limited periods in a familiar situation and will soon be able to function without direct help in a bigger group.

The foundations of the child's independence are becoming established.

Growth, not pathology: the central tenet

Nurture groups are about children's learning; they are not therapy. The focus of intervention for psychotherapists is the children's difficulties, and their concern is to unravel knots in a tangled fabric of early experience. The thrust of the work of the nurture practitioners is different: it is the process and content of normal early emotional, social and cognitive development, and the relationships, experiences and physical environment that support and facilitate this. They are concerned with weaving in and strengthening the strands of early nurture. Their perspective is forward-looking from birth, not looking back from the present. The process is one of normal learning, it is education, but at an earlier-than-usual level and the challenge is to build in the emotional, social and cognitive developmental experiences inherent in early nurture. As practitioners become confident in the approach, the mood in the school changes from despair to optimism and hope as school staff no longer feel de-skilled but become empowered.

Attachment

The process in the nurture group, as in families, is based in and through attachment (Bowlby, 1969), and is mediated within and through a secure relationship (Ainsworth, 1978). It is a complex process, but under benign circumstances, it happens during the course of normal parenting, intuitively, without much conscious thought. To restore this process in the nurture group, it is crucial that the children become attached. Their needs then become apparent, the adults respond accordingly, and the learning process follows. Some children do not attach and respond; these need more than the nurture group can provide. Becoming attached, and all that follows from this, depends on re-creating the structure as well as the content of the earliest years.

A model of normal development and parenting

The nurture practitioners provide a normal learning experience of the earliest years by responding intuitively to the children, as parents do. (See Earliest learning: a summary chart). They build up incrementally their experience of themselves and the world, and positive relationships with others. The process is structured overall by an explicit awareness of the nature and content of development, the context that is essential to it, and its direct relevance to the work of the mainstream class. It is a total learning experience, and is the earliest stage of the normal developmental/educational continuum. Practice, intuitively and in conceptual analysis, is based on normal development in the first three years, structured in discussion and developed as a nurture curriculum leading into the appropriate level for the child of the EYFS and National Curriculum.

The classic nurture group and some variants

A classic nurture group is a class, typically of 10 to 12 children, staffed by a teacher and teaching assistant. It is in the child's neighbourhood primary school and is an integral part of the school. The classroom is furnished to be both home and school, is comfortable and welcoming, containing and protected. It is big enough for a wide range of domestic and personal activities including 'breakfast' early in the day and needed experiences at the 0–3 developmental level, as well as activities that lead into and overlap with the EYFS/ KS1 curriculum and opportunity for the appropriate age-related level of the National Curriculum. Children will be on the register of their mainstream class group and will be included in any class activities that they can manage successfully. From the beginning, they join their class for registration, assembly, break and lunchtimes and spend half a day a week in the classroom. The class teacher remains the responsible teacher for overseeing the child's learning and progress, with curriculum planning and assessment being a shared, collaborative responsibility. There is a continuous flow of communication between the child's class teacher and the nurture staff.

'Nurture'

The word has a specific, meaningful and purposeful connotation; it describes the children's needs, the nature of the help provided and the learning experiences involved. The class is therefore referred to as the nurture group but is known in school according to the system in use, for example 'rainbow class'.

Some variants

Nurture group practitioners quickly saw possibilities for adapting and applying the underlying principles of the original model more widely. Some schools modified classroom practice and whole-school policies to create a more nurturing ethos generally throughout the school, recognizing that when the needs of the most vulnerable children are met, then all children benefit and standards overall will rise.

With the resurgence in interest in nurture groups, we are seeing even more innovative applications of the principles both in the UK and internationally. These may be flexible variations on the part-time group, groups for older children in Key Stages 2 and 3, the application to other settings such as PRUs (or short-term schools) and special EBD schools or as a shared resource between a group of schools.

Nurture Groups in Quebec

'Kangaroo' classes started during 2005–6 in Quebec, Canada. Some also take children with severe behavioural difficulties and/or mental health problems, for whom there is no appropriate provision. They are based in a regular elementary school, have about seven students with a teacher and a teaching assistant and practice is based on nurture group principles (Bennathan and Boxall, 2000). They have a more therapeutic and less preventive approach than the UK model and students come from different schools within a school board district. Some are geographically distant from their neighbourhood school and do not have contact with their original class, although special efforts are made to allow them to spend time in regular classes. The essential features are maintained: physical organization, the understanding of the children's difficulties and how they are managed, the routines and structure. The initiative has had a great impact on the life of the children and their families. Many children who previously needed home tuition have now attended regular school happily for the whole year. The model has proved so effective in Quebec that many other school boards have set up groups, with some developing the model in secondary schools for 'grown-up kangaroos'.

Caroline Couture
email: caroline.couture1@UQTR.ca
Caroline is Professor in the Centre de recherche et d'intervention sur la réussite scolaire (CRIRES), Department of Psychoeducation, Université du Québec à Trois-Rivières.

Whether or not such groups may rightly be termed nurture groups depends on how closely they adhere to the underlying principles. Cooper and Whitebread (2007) identify four variants but not all are authentic nurture groups. The curriculum is the essential identifying feature; children are not withdrawn from the curriculum but it is modified to enable them to engage in it at their appropriate developmental level.

The nurture group principles

• Children's learning is understood developmentally.
• It is understood that all behaviour is communication.
• The classroom offers a safe space.
• Nurture is important for the development of self-esteem.
• Language is a vital means of communication.
• The importance of transitions in children's lives is understood.

(Lucas et al., 2006)

These principles are an objective indicator to help schools determine the required elements of nurture group provision and to support curriculum planning. They are used prudently within the essential intuitive, relational and holistic nature of the provision for children at an early developmental level as described below and in which they are implicit.

Re-creating the process of earliest learning

The notion that they should respond intuitively to children is usually attractive to the nurture practitioners, and the term 'nurture' is likely to suggest a close, supportive and caring relationship. Additionally, at this early stage in the home, experiences for babies and toddlers are determined and limited by their perceptual and motor development and physiological rhythm. In recreating this learning process in school, the adults must ensure that the children's day is equivalent to that of the first three years at home as described in Part 2. The nurture group thus provides a restorative experience of early nurture as the first stage of the learning/educational process.

The working model

The adults provide a complex learning experience of inter-meshing emotional, social and cognitive developmental strands by being fully available to the children, as parents are. They respond intuitively to any behaviour that would be normal in very young children. To make their task manageable, a general principle was adopted and this continues to be the guideline: 'We will be and do for them as we would for our own, at whatever developmental level they appear to be.' This leads directly to concerned identification with the children and an uncondi-tional commitment to their well-being. It gives confidence and provides a working model that generates management strategies and learning experiences that are purposeful and of crucial developmental importance.

The school and parents

School is local, accessible and familiar. The staff make friendly supportive relationships with the parents, who sometimes ask for practical advice, and when distressed are given time and attention. They feel valued for themselves, not just because they are the par-ents of the children. This is a positive factor in their children's progress in school and their well-being at home.

The nurture group is fully integrated within a supportive school

The purpose of the group is to enable the children to be fully part of their peer group within a year or, at most, four terms. The group functions as an integral part of the school, as in addition to achieving and relating productively to each other, the children need help to extend their growing competence. They see and begin to make viable relationships in wider contexts and move outwards with confidence because they feel themselves to be at the protected centre of widening networks of support.

The adults' responsibilities therefore extend to creating an inte-grated experience for the children that includes the world of school beyond the group. Procedures within the school are modi-fied and thus offer a nurturing environment that includes the entire school community and even beyond, providing the child with a positive, reinforcing and sustained experience and contributing to community cohesion (DCSF, 2007a). The interacting and cumulatively developing process that is the substance of nurture work thus mirrors the normal human situation at social as well as personal levels.

Size of group

The developmental needs of some of the children are not apparent in an individual relationship, and although individual work consolidates and reinforces an attachment, opportunities do not arise naturally to help them to separate and function autonomously within the peer group. Nearly all the children need to learn to give and take with others and to be self-directing, and so it is essential that they are in groups where they are required to respect the needs and attitudes of others. In the early groups, 12 children was found to be a viable number to offer a broad enough range of opportunities for making relationships (see Chapter 9).

The teacher and assistant partnership

Two people are needed to run the group; a classic group requires a teacher and a teaching assistant, partly for the mutual support and personal development this provides but also because the children need to see constructive interaction between adults. The adults work closely together in a mutually supportive, interdependent partnership, there is considerable overlap of roles and each may take the lead at different times. The teacher takes primary responsibility for curriculum planning, assessment and recording of progress and liaison with others within the school and beyond, but both play a crucial role in creating the safe and secure environment in which children flourish and their learning is enhanced (Frederickson and Cline, 2002).

Using the model of normal learning in the earliest years with its intuitive sense of the child's early developmental needs and the parent–baby/toddler interactive process, the adults ensure that experiences and events are relevant and are simple, unhurried and carefully planned and controlled. At Key Stage (KS) 3, the roles resemble those of mentors (Cooper, 2001) or learning coaches (Claxton, 2002).

The structure and content of the day

The nurture day is structured to be appropriate for the level of personal organization and control of a young child: the pace is slower, the structure tighter and the constraints more immediate and evident than in the mainstream class, all essential for unhurried early developmental learning. It also reinforces trust and security, underpins the purposeful direction of behaviour and events, and provides a context for the National Curriculum. Within this structure, the children can be let go into baby/toddler-level activities or drawn back into an early attachment relationship.

The context is supportive, and through their relationship with the adults, they gain:

- trust and security
- awareness of their own feelings and those of others
- visual and kinaesthetic awareness of themselves, leading to a more integrated and differentiated body image
- increasing awareness of their own bodies in space
- awareness of the sensory qualities of the things about them, and their relationships
- appropriate and purposeful attention to their immediate real world
- communication and language skills.

These experiences are the essential underpinnings of all later development, that is:

- the capacity for empathy
- control and management of their own bodies
- attention-giving and achievement
- a more coherent understanding of the properties of the physical world and of sequence and process
- constructive social relationships and conversation.

All this leads to more effective use of their formal learning opportunities, increasing self-worth and a sense of mastery and control of events.

The learning process for the adults

The process has considerable learning potential for the adults, for they live through the experience with the children and at the same time are explicitly aware of the developmental content and its relevance to the requirements of the mainstream class. They are therefore intellectually and emotionally involved and gain theoretical insights as well as considerable personal awareness and enrichment. Their commitment and resourcefulness are at a high level and they have little need to turn to others for support.

The adults initiate and foster this growth process by 'feeling into' the earliest years and identifying with the feelings and needs of the children. It is a human response, and the most valuable source of help for the adults is within themselves.

They draw on their own intuitive resources and each learns from the other. In discussion with other nurture group practitioners, they deepen their perception of themselves in relation to the children, and gain increasing understanding of the emotional and cognitive content of their work. They are reassured of the validity of their intuitive response (Furlong, 2000) and begin to discipline this within a simple and clearly formulated developmental framework that leads, in concept and in practice, to the expectations and aims of the mainstream class. This approach dissipates the anxiety and impotence generated by the children's difficulties, provides a helpful guideline, and frees the adults to draw fully on their own personal resources, uninhibited by the feeling that somewhere there are 'experts' who know better.

The teacher's role: managing experiences

This process depends on a close relationship with the children and an intuitive 'feel' of their needs, but there are reservations:

- The process for children in the years before school is carried forward by an innate impetus for growth, but in the nurture group, it is the teacher's responsibility to know where the process is leading and to provide direction.
- The experiences of children aged 0–3 are determined and constrained by their developing physical competence and come to in an ordered and incremental way with all aspects intermesh-

ing. For older children in the nurture group, the teacher has to provide the constraints, plan comparable experiences, focus the children's attention on them, and provide and support the necessary repetition. This presupposes that the teacher has sufficient faith in the rationale of the approach to be committed to the tight structuring that is needed.

- The teacher therefore needs, more than the interested parent, an explicit awareness of the nature of the developmental process, the circumstances that are essential to it, and its direct relevance to the work of the mainstream class.

The nurture group leads to a nurturing school

The work of the nurture group always involves the class teachers concerned, and in a committed school or group of schools, all staff are nurturing in attitude, have some understanding of the needs of the children in the group and actively support their development. In schools where there are considerable numbers of vulnerable children, the principles underpinning nurture work are incorporated into school policies and become part of general classroom practice. This requires the nurture group to be well established, the underlying principles to be accepted and their relevance to normal academic achievement to be understood. The first step, therefore, towards a cumulatively reinforcing nurturing process in the school generally is to have a classic nurture group, running well. But an essential determinant of eventual integration of the children within the mainstream class is the initial and continuing involvement of the class teachers in understanding and supporting the work of the group. As with the development of the children, this is a circular, reinforcing and ultimately spiralling process. It is a whole-school responsibility; it takes patience and time for the many strands in this intermeshing and reinforcing process to come together and for the work to be seen as successful.

Reversing the downwards spiral of deprivation

Making explicit the implicit learning content of earliest childhood led us into an area that was little explored at the time (in the 1970s). Nurture groups and the growth and health of the children within them owe everything to the goodwill, generosity and self-less work of all concerned. Each has generated energy and enthusiasm for the others. Each has relied on a personal capacity to cope, but the knowledge that others were in the same position provided support; the shared problem-solving contributed to the foundations on which everyone has built. The work itself is energizing. It is implicitly an affirmation of a commitment to life and brings increasing self-awareness and the energizing sense of shared growth. All these things are found in good measure in the nurture groups, and we have good reason to believe that the children and their families have gained as much from us as we have from them.

Around the time of the first nurture groups, Sir Keith Joseph, then Secretary of State for Education, coined the phrase 'The cycle of deprivation'. Now, 40 years on, the lives of many families continue to be blighted by stress (Layard and Dunn, 2009). Despite government policies, deprivation is still a downwards and inwardly spiralling process of despair and depression; nurture is an upwards and outwardly spiralling process of hope and growth. We believe that the investment of our capital of good nurture for the future is of the utmost importance.

It would be logical to make this provision available at the earliest stage to all children and young people at risk of personal and school failure, and the disastrous future that so often lies ahead.

Summary ☐

- Nurture groups are a proven intervention for emotionally vulnerable children and young people; they contribute to raising standards and are cost-effective.

- Children's needs are complex and varied but the approach is a positive one, drawing on the intuitive response of the adults to relate to the child at a developmentally appropriate level.

- Nurture groups are about children's learning; although primarily an early intervention strategy, the principles are valid for children and young people of different ages and in different settings.

- Nurture groups are at the centre of a network of relationships in the school and beyond and contribute to the well-being of society and to community cohesion.

Further reading

Claxton, G. (2002) *Building Learning Power: Helping Young People Become Better Learners.* Bristol: TLO. Nurture practitioners/learning coaches or mentors, working with young people in KS3/4, will find Guy Claxton's 4 Rs – resilience, resourcefulness, reflection and relationships – a helpful vocabulary for communicating nurture principles.

Geddes, H. (2006) *Attachment in the Classroom.* London: Worth Publishing. This is an accessible book on attachment theory for use with school governors, senior leaders and staff generally.

Layard, R. and Dunn, J. (2009) *A Good Childhood: Searching for Values in a Competitive Age.* London: Children's Society. This book describes the obstacles that children face in today's society and which impact on their well-being and learning.

2

40 Years On: New Research and Nurture Groups

> **This chapter considers:**
> - the current context for nurture groups within statutory educational provision
> - developments in educational practice and pedagogy
> - new research in developmental psychology and neuroscience relevant to nurture group practice
> - the future of the Nurture Group Network.

The lifetime of nurture groups, the past 40 years, has seen rapid progress in developmental psychology and neuroscience. This is having a major impact on our understanding of early development and its importance for later life and is a powerful affirmation of nurture practice.

The context

Developments within the structures of pre-school and statutory educational provision over recent years provide new routes to intervention in the education of children vulnerable to SEBD. The Every Child Matters agenda of the Children's Plan (DCSF, 2007b) is now central and the five outcomes accord well with the aims of nurture groups. All schools are required to address Every Child Matters in their policies and improvement plans and Ofsted

inspections report on how well this is being achieved. Government intervention includes the provision of Sure Start children's
centres for the pre-school years, bringing together early education,
childcare, health and family support aimed particularly at disadvantaged families and the Behaviour and Education Support
Programme (BEST) for schools facing specific difficulties.
Children's centres are now government policy and the problem of
'fade out' on admission to school is recognized (Wood and
Caulier-Grice, 2006). The Early Years Foundation Stage (EYFS) and
the National Curriculum have been revised and further revision of
the primary curriculum is due in 2011; assessment procedures are
under review to allow more flexibility to teachers in addressing
children's needs. The Lamb inquiry into SEN and parental confidence (DCSF, 2009b) and further guidance on the extended
schools' programme are in progress. All these initiatives are
included in the recent White Paper 'Your Child, Your Schools, Our
Future: building a 21st Century School System' (DCSF, 2009b). The
emphasis particularly on early intervention and coherent children's services working with clusters of schools has potential
benefits for children who need nurture group provision.

All these developments impinge in some way on nurture
group work. Intuition and spontaneity in responding to children's needs will continue to be crucially important in nurture
group practice and the starting point for intervention but, in
order to be sustainable in the present education system, intuition must be backed up with a knowledge and understanding
of the context in which schools operate and nurture work must
be grounded in sound theory.

Pedagogy

The first generation of nurture group teachers in the UK were familiar with aspects of child development and psychology as part of their
teacher training courses in the 1950s and 1960s, notably Bowlby's
Child Care and the Growth of Love (1953) as a key text (University of
Durham, 1956–8). They continued to be informed by theories of
child development current at the time, e.g. Piaget, Donaldson,
Bruner and later Chomsky and Vygotsky (Liverpool Institute of

Higher Education: Notre Dame College, 1975–9). Insley and Lucas (2009) and others drew on this professional knowledge within the intuitive approach of nurture group practice which gave them 'permission' to make the relational and affective aspects of teaching through a close parent–child relationship, the priority.

This knowledge has now entered the repertoire for all teachers and also increasingly teaching assistants and mentors through new opportunities for professional development. Terms such as: demonstrating, modelling, scaffolding and 'withitness' used by developmental psychologists to conceptualize aspects of adult/child interaction are now familiar criteria for good teaching and the interactions they articulate are no longer the prerogative of nurture practitioners. The descriptive accounts which follow in later chapters illustrate these now familiar terms which find their origins within the responsive parent–child relationship.

Nurture group practitioners, as action researchers (see, for example, Altrichter et al., 2008; Loughran et al., 2002; Somekh, 2006) and in their professional development, continue to be encouraged to reflect on the new insights and build on and apply them to their previous knowledge and understanding. They know, and are committed to, what the evidence of psychologists now supports unreservedly: that the intuitive ways of relating to – and teaching – children as individuals according to their developmental level rather than some arbitrary age-related level, is the way to healthy psychological growth and educational achievement. It is not about a set of learned behaviours but a two-way process, a dynamic relationship between people. This is at the heart of nurture group practice – and we would say of all good pedagogy – which must never be reduced to a prescribed, off-the-shelf programme of tasks to be achieved.

Developmental psychology

Bowlby's pioneering work (1953, 1969) in which he studied the bonding process of parents and their children is now well known as attachment theory and is the theoretical base for nurture group practice. Importantly for practitioners who aim to establish a close relationship with children modelled on that of parent–child, the theory emphasizes the behaviours and cognitive structures which go into maintaining this relationship over time.

Other psychologists went on to investigate different aspects of attachment. Ainsworth (1978) studied the quality of the attachments and how different patterns of insecure attachments develop, underlining the importance of a secure base. Later, Crittenden (1992) identified problems associated with 'anxiously attached children during infancy and pre-school years' (p. 575) who, unless helped, become troubled adolescents. Important for nurture practitioners is her observation that 'intense emotional arousal' (p. 580) may be modified by a carer's sensitivity to children's needs; they fail to learn how to deal with their emotions if management is insensitive. She suggests that anxiously attached children 'intuitively' discern the effects of their behaviour: as a child rejects or reacts, the carer's response informs, and may even support, the inappropriate behaviour which then becomes a coercive strategy: insecurely attached 'anxious' children may have parents and grandparents in the same state, perpetuating the cycle, and having implication for work with families: 'In all cases of anxious attachment, there are two hurt individuals, the child and the attachment figure.' (p. 600).

Trevarthen (1977) concentrated on what strengthens attachment. His research focused on the interactions between mothers and their babies, studying particularly the way in which they cooperate and engage in face-to-face communication and how their facial expressions, gestures, touch and the sounds they make, mirror each other.

Since the study of the effects of severe deprivation on the Romanian orphans (Rutter, 1998) recently, psychologists have focused more on the effects of environment than on genetic inheritance in understanding children's later difficulties – the nature/nurture debate. 'Just as everything about our minds is caused by our brains, everything about our brains is ultimately caused by our evolutionary history ... for human beings, nurture *is* our nature (Gopnik, 1999: 8). Findings which are of particular relevance for nurture work are:

• Schore (1993), going further than Trevarthan, suggests that positive looks and smiles actually promote brain development:

they are 'the most vital stimulus to the growth of the social, emotionally intelligent brain' (Gerhardt, 2004: 41).

- Babies and young children develop 'internalized working models' which influence their expectation of future relationships but, importantly, these can be modified. 'Even abused children often seem to escape long-lasting damage if there is somebody around who does not turn away. A relatively brief experience of a friend or an aunt or a teacher can provide children with an alternative picture of how love can work' (Gopnik et al., 1999: 49).

- There is great importance in these other attachment relationships and especially in fathers who play with their children (Grossman et al., 2005).

What is becoming ever clearer to nurture practitioners through recent research is the crucial importance of the earliest developmental stages in laying the foundations for all successful future learning and that this applies not only to younger primary school children but also to older children, young people and adults. Attachment is no longer thought to be merely biological; it is not:

> a once-and-for-all event that must take place in a critical period. Knowledge guides emotion more than emotion distorts knowledge. The relations between parents and children, like all human relations, develop and change as both partners come to know and understand each other better. (Gopnik et al., 1999: 48–9).

Nor is being a parent essential: 'Every new thing we learn about babies tells us something new about us; we are, after all, only babies who have been around for a while' (Gopnik et al., 1999: 22). Our insights into children and young people's needs and desires, perceptions and emotions owe as much to our own experience as to any parental/practitioner role.

Developments in neuroscience

For nurture groups, focused interest in the work of neuroscience began in 2000 with an invitation, from Professor Susan Greenfield, to attend a seminar on learning and the brain at the Royal Institution (Boxall et al., 2000). We realized that the way in which children's brains developed had always been important in our work.

The early nurture groups had drawn on Elinor Goldschmied's work with the Treasure Basket (Goldschmied and Jackson, 2004, 1994). Much has happened since 2000. The boundaries between the disciplines are now less clearly defined; child neuroscience is an emerging discipline (Reed and Warner-Rogers, 2008) and while it has much to contribute to education, neuroscientists urge caution when applying findings from adult neuroscience (which is mainly concerned with responding to brain damage as a result of accident or illness) to children. Educationalists, too, have been cautious of jumping to conclusions on the basis of limited research (McNeil, 1999) although many of these earlier fears have not been realized and the positive advantages for enhancing learning are now being recognized (McNeil, 2008).

Reservations apart, what neuroscientists can tell us about the development of the brain is tremendously affirming of intuitive nurture group practice – and we would hope for education more widely.

> The new perspective is not due to any single breakthrough but to the remarkable impact of many things happening at once, in neuroscience, psychology, psychoanalysis, biochemistry. As these disciplines begin to communicate and to influence each other, they are offering a deeper understanding of how human beings become fully human and how they relate emotionally to others ... by understanding human infancy and the developments of the 'social brain' and the biological systems involved in emotional regulation. (Gerhardt, 2004: 2)

We now know that the developing brain is highly energetic and flexible and is not fixed at birth but continues to grow as the child explores the world. Every experience, thought and action creates or breaks neural connections at an unprecedented rate. Before birth, up to a quarter of a million new cells grow every minute, making 1.8 million connections per second, though many of these later wither and die unless reinforced with use. During the first year, the brain doubles in weight. Research using MRI (magnetic resonance imaging) strongly suggests that how children are cared for, i.e. loved, actually affects the size of the brain areas and influences the brain's maturation process (Teicher et al., 2003). Gerhardt (2004) describes the baby's biochemical responses to smell, touch and sound and, later, visual stimuli – positive looks – which contribute to the development of their nervous system and the brain through their relationship with others. 'The kind of brain each baby develops is the brain that comes out of his or her particular experiences with people ... our brains are socially programmed by the older members of our community, so that we adapt to the particular family and social group we must live among' (Gerhardt, 2004: 38).

We now know that learning, memory and language begin before birth. It is clear that any damage to the developing brain *in utero* through alcohol and drug misuse in pregnancy can have serious consequences, as does maternal stress. Plasticity, the ability of the brain to recover and change itself in the light of new experience, suggests that any damage done has the possibility of recovery in the right environment (Gopnik et al., 2009; Greenfield, 2000).

Children's early years through to the end of primary school are a time of rapid brain growth and neural connections are re-inforced through repetition, a crucial aspect of nurture group practice; every experience has an effect and contributes to the adult they will become. Between six months and a year old, the frontal lobes become more active, triggering the development of the emotions, attachments, planning, working memory and attention. A sense of self develops around 18 months and a sense of other people having their own minds at 3–4 years. Adverse life experiences in these critical years may have a lasting effect on a person's ability to cope with stress in later life.

The brain is 95% of its adult weight by the age of six and at its peak of energy consumption. In a healthy environment, children start to apply logic and trust and to understand their own thought processes. Their brains continue to grow and make and break connections until puberty, around 11 for girls and 14 for boys.

By adolescence, brains may be fully grown but are still undergoing major structural changes as some neural connections mature and others die. Those associated with sensory and motor areas mature first, then language and spatial orientation and lastly the area associated with control of impulses, judgement and decision-making. At this stage, there is amazing potential for new learning given the right opportunities, but the lack of impulse control can be a serious problem and requires careful management, as practitioners well know.

Intuition

Bruner interprets intuition as 'going beyond' (1960). He maintains that it is one of a loose-knit family of 'ways of knowing' which are less articulated and explicit than normal reasoning and discourse and which have been marginalized in mainstream education. Our modern culture perceives intuition and imagination to lack a cognitive psychological basis which makes scientific sense but, by its nature, intuitive practice is reflective and requires judgement (Claxton, 2000; Pollard, 2002). Reflection has always been an essential element in nurture group practice; it is at the root of the Boxall Profile (see Chapters 3 to 5). Nurture teachers, in their teacher–assistant partnerships and at their meetings together, reflected on their relationships with the children and one another and, rather than responding to the prevailing 'wisdom', they developed the practice we have today. Intuition and reflection continue to be areas requiring further study; they are closely linked to the need for an understanding of how best to support practitioners who carry the responsibility for the future well-being of our most vulnerable children and young people.

The Nurture Group Network

The Nurture Group Network is the charity established in 2005 to promote the development of nurture groups and which is developing an important strategic role. It currently provides a range of excellent professional development in partnership with a number of local authorities (LAs) and also liaises with three universities to provide postgraduate courses in nurture work. There is now a well-informed workforce running more than 1000 groups in the UK and abroad. There are emerging opportunities arising from recent government reports (Rose, 2009; Steer, 2009) to have more prominence within policy. Funding will continue to be an issue so long as nurture group provision is seen to be an optional extra rather than essential to inclusion.

The possible future role for LAs as commissioners of services rather than providers will be an impetus to the development of the Nurture Group Network as a Centre of Excellence. The Marjorie Boxall Quality Mark which sets and requires evidence of the basic standards to be met by a school is already well established.

The outcomes of the Cambridge research project (Cooper and Whitebread, 2007) have provided valuable evidence and identified clear principles and key characteristics to support the promotion of nurture groups. There will be new opportunities for research as children's emotional and behavioural needs continue to be more clearly defined and teachers' conceptual analysis is further developed. The contribution of nurture groups to promoting community cohesion and social mobility is another emerging and valuable area for study.

Nurture groups practitioners have played an invaluable, if low key, part in the development of education over the past 40 years. They have demonstrated a commitment to fundamental beliefs and principles about the entitlement to high-quality education for every child that predates Every Child Matters, and they believe passionately that this is achievable when there is a balance between both qualitative and quantitative aspects of education, when the relational and affective matter as much as the measurable. This is the challenge for the next generation.

Summary ☐

- The development of the theory and practice within Nurture Groups is dynamic and ongoing.
- Whatever political changes occur, practitioners are at the forefront: they are the agents in developing provision to meet the needs of vulnerable children and young people.
- Nurture Groups work and the principles work in different settings: much has been achieved and will endure.

Further reading

Altrichter, H., Feldman, A., Posch, P. and Somekh, B. (2008) *Teachers Investigate Their Work: An Introduction to Action Research Across the Professions*, 2nd edition. London: Routledge. This book is a useful, practical starter to action research. It is also possible to study the methodology through courses such as *Teacher as Researcher: Exploring*

Issues and Contexts (Institute of Education, University of London: www.ioe.ac.uk).

Gerhardt, S. (2004) *Why Love Matters: How Affection Shapes a Baby's Brain.* Hove: Brunner-Routledge. Writing on brain research is growing rapidly and this book is especially recommended.

James, A. and James, A. (2008) *Key Concepts in Childhood Studies.* London: Sage. This is a useful book which explores the key ideas behind childhood studies.

Wheatley, M. (2002) *Turning to One Another: Simple Conversations to Restore Hope to the Future.* San Francisco, CA: Berrett-Koehler. In this book, the author explores ways of communicating with one another. See www.turningtooneanother.net

Part 2

NURTURE GROUPS
IN ACTION

Part 2 goes to the heart of nurture group practice. Chapters 3 to 5 describe the structures and practice which grew from nurture practitioners' observations, the origin of the Boxall Profile. Chapters 6 and 7 focus on the learning which forms the nurture curriculum.

3

The Organization of Experience

This chapter explains how:

- the needs of children and young people are identified and understood through close observation
- the Boxall Profile is the starting point for intervention
- attention to detail, routines and repetition build in and reinforce attachment and support
- the concept of group is established
- structuring the way ahead leads to achievement.

Many children and young people are without the personal resources needed for school and are a major problem for their teachers (Daniels and Williams, 2000). To varying extents, their past experience, personal organization and self-control are poor, and they have insufficient awareness and understanding of their surroundings to give purposeful attention.

Some give their whole attention to anticipated attack, and become aggressive or have a tantrum if accidentally touched. Others are bewildered and inattentive and make no response to requests. Others again are confused, have no sense of self or purposeful, meaningful action and hold back, not able to involve themselves. Others yet again are tense, tightly controlled and organized, but very restricted in what they can do, and are without spontaneity and initiative. Some sit awkwardly and do not spontaneously involve themselves, while a few seem out of touch with their surroundings and occasionally might rock. Many interfere with children nearby, indiscriminately and trivially. Others are exuberant with energy, stretch out, loll and roll about and disturb the others, and when an activity is initiated, they rush in without waiting to grasp what is expected, and with no understanding of what they are to do. Another child might sit hunched up, half turned away. He is sullen and resentful and reacts negatively or angrily to all requests, and particularly if older is likely to be hostile and alienated, and has no wish or intention of being involved. Some do take part to some extent but are poorly organized and unhappy, restless and resistive; others are listless and without interest, and have no appetite for experiences. In general, they are not biddable and few spontaneously make eye contact, particularly at the beginning of the day. If they attend at all, it is rarely to the teacher as a person, or purposefully to an object or event as a complete whole. They notice little of what is happening, other people have little relevance for them, and they do not engage purposefully with the situation or use toys and materials constructively. Teachers sense that underlying these difficulties is a history of disappointment and failure, and the expectation of continuing disappointment and failure. The children are likely to remain inattentive and unsettled. There is no sense of group, no interaction with each other and no expectancy in relation to the teacher.

All behaviour is communication; close observation is the key to knowing where to begin.

The Boxall Profile

The Boxall Profile (Bennathan and Boxall, 1998) is the instrument used in nurture groups to structure observation of children and to provide objective data to support the teacher's intuitive judgement that these children would be good candidates for a nurture group. The pattern of scores indicates their underlying needs for attachment and early learning experiences in order to organize their experience. The focus is on progress within the Developmental Strands of the Boxall Profile to ensure that these basic needs are being met. Whatever their chronological age, the children need to:

- give purposeful attention
- participate constructively
- connect up experiences
- show insightful involvement
- engage cognitively with peers.

The Boxall Profile enables nurture group practitioners to identify the starting point for intervention and learning for each individual child within the overall organization of the nurture group.

Attachment and support

The nurture teacher's objective is to attach the children and provide support for clearly defined and manageable expectations and goals. This enables them to achieve. Security and attachment are bound into this process and from simple achievements stem the development of basic knowledge, skills and competencies necessary for participation in the mainstream class summed up in the developmental strands. Routine is the broad structure for this process. Procedures vary from school to school and will to some extent depend on the age of the children, although the fundamental principles remain the same. The same routine is followed in the same way, every day, and, except for unavoidable events, the same familiar people are in the same expected place, every day.

Establishing daily routines

From the moment children arrive on the school site, they need to be 'held' in a network of support. This goes beyond the level of general supervision and is important because many of the children are confused about their surroundings or are indiscriminately attracted by irrelevant events; they are poorly organized within themselves, have a high level of anxiety and are unlikely to have had a reassuring and supportive start to the day. Children who arrive early may attend a breakfast or out-of-school club. Other children are welcomed a few minutes before school begins by the adult who is supervising in the playground. For all of them, their first personal welcome is from the nurture staff. This first contact with a familiar and reassuring presence is the beginning of systematic and reinforcing support throughout the school day.

Registration in the mainstream class is usual practice as this provides a regular contact that is manageable for all but a few out-of-touch or particularly alienated children. They wait to be collected by the nurture teacher or assistant who provides a visible link with the class teacher and continuity of attachment. They exchange friendly appreciative comments about the children that convey their expectations. Children who cannot register in their mainstream class are received and welcomed by the assistant in the nurture classroom, and the teacher collects the others in an orderly routine. The children are 'contained'. A child particularly in need of support walks hand in hand with the adult. The adult chooses the order in which they are to walk, because at this stage they push, fight and argue if not given clear directives. They are reminded to walk well, and to carry their coats and other possessions tidily. Constant positive reminders are necessary because the children cannot regulate their own behaviour; they have not internalized order and initially need order to be imposed. The children wait at the door of their classroom in the order already established, without jostling each other. They are reminded not to rush and to go in only when everyone is quiet and still.

In some schools, all the children come directly to the nurture group. The adults are already there. One of them is available to chat with any parents who come and occasionally a parent stays on. The other is available for the children.

Children who cannot register in their mainstream classes come directly to the nurture group; they do not have the stabilizing routine of walking to the group room in an orderly way and waiting quietly before they go in. Latecomers miss these early routines and need help to latch in.

Help with every detail

Some nurture teachers take groups of children to the nurture classroom as they collect them. The assistant is waiting, welcomes them, and helps them to hang their coats on the right peg. This is a clearly delineated task that indirectly controls the children's behaviour by focusing their attention on themselves and on the task of hanging up their coats. It also provides positive direction by preventing the disorganization and disruption that arises if they cannot decide which peg to choose or want someone else's. The pegs might be colour-coded to their mainstream class, with an individual's name and photograph on it. This provides a link with their mainstream class, acknowledges their identity and introduces them to symbolic representation. One group began the day by walking from the door of the classroom heel to toe along a line marked on the floor, one of the adults going first. In another, children walked in on numbered footsteps painted on the floor, counting as they went.

All this attention to detail concentrates the children's attention on themselves in a purposeful way and gives vital practice in motor coordination and balance. It is a particularly useful beginning to the day because many have little awareness of their own bodies, and are poorly coordinated. The first children to arrive choose an activity from a strictly limited range in the home area if they are able, otherwise they wait with one adult while the rest of the group are assembling.

Registration

Although most children will have registered already in their mainstream class, there is always a less formal registration in the nurture group. The procedure adopted is the same each day and carries important learning experiences. For example, children find their individual name card, which might have their photograph on the back, from a box of cards or from a scatter on the table, and put it in the appropriate wall pocket. The pockets are in numbered order from left to right and they use the next empty one, or are required to put it in a pocket in the colour of the mainstream class, or the one with their name or photograph. This exercise provides an experience of sorting, identifying, matching and filing, and movement from left to right, and sequence. Help with this basic task is given for as long as they need it.

A manageable, ritualized routine

The ritualized routine that begins the day is a simple, manageable

procedure that slows them down and calms them. It is a recognizable beginning to the day, is remembered and becomes familiar
and reassuring. It gives each child the satisfaction of a task
achieved, and the satisfaction of approval. Putting a name card
into the wall pocket is an objective representation that is both tan-
gible and symbolic of their identity, their presence in the school
and membership of the group. They are anchored firmly in the
group, and the beginning of the day has been marked.

The home area: the secure place

The children move to the home area and face the teacher. The area
is established as a safe place, first by controlling where they sit;
young children are given a designated place on the carpet, thus
avoiding arguments, while older children may sit on personal
cushions or chairs in a circle. Some have a poor sense of their bodies in space, as though without sufficient experience of free
movement, and are confused and poorly orientated. If necessary,
they are taken by the hand and guided to a place. Many have little or no structure of their own, no grasp of where the situation is
leading or what is expected, and without this help continue to be
confused and disorganized. Those who are particularly without
experience and volition, and remain passive and unresponsive,
may need individual help to sit appropriately and comfortably in
the required place; a verbal request is not sufficient. Others
respond to instructions and one or two are able to find a place on
their own.

The simple, quiet, slow-moving and familiar routines of the
home area create a sense of security and children are brought back
here during the day whenever they are becoming fretful or arguments are breaking out, or the noise and excitement level are
rising. At these times, all activities are stopped and the teacher
'brings them back', as parents do with young children, to reassure
them that they are there and all is well; the teacher 'lets them go'
again when they are once more able to manage on their own.

Group time in the home area is important, because the children
are learning to relate to the teacher and to be physically part of a
group without any requirement to be involved with the others.
The teacher judges their mood and competence during group

activities, and the extent to which their attention can be gained and held. The day's activities and expectations are modified accordingly and spelt out for them.

The home area is also the place where 'being biddable' is re-inforced. Bringing the children together in the home area several times during the day maintains close reassuring physical proxim-ity to the teacher, and encourages eye contact in a comforting and supportive situation. It also builds in the expectation that the adults' wishes will be heeded and they will be pleased. Sometimes these wishes are demonstrated more visibly.

> At the beginning of the year, the children had quickly begun to meet the teacher's requirements at their regular snack time, but were not otherwise readily biddable. The routine and ritualized occasion of snack and fruit continued, but the teacher now gathered the children together two or three times a day, and they all had a piece of fruit. The next step was to call the children together for a little pleasurable group activity and then disperse them again, without giving them fruit. In this way, the 'being biddable' response was strengthened and extended, and became part of the growing relationship with the teacher.

Attending

Some teachers specify how children are to sit, for example with their legs crossed, arms folded and hands tucked away, lips together and their eyes on them. The children associate this requirement with giving attention to the teacher, and because everyone is doing the same thing, everyone's attention is re-inforced. Because they are concentrating on self-control, they are less likely to fidget and interfere with the others. They know they have these four things to remember. Teachers have stressed the value and importance of having a clear expectation. Others require the children to be contained and attentive, sit still and wait. If there is enough room, the assistant sits with the children and the teacher faces them. The children feel supported because the assistant sits with them and joins in the activity. The adults might exchange roles at a later stage.

It is time to begin. The children are in the home area, facing the teacher, who is alert to potential trouble. The children are positioned carefully and a young child might be brought closer or another moved to a different place in the group. Many of them actively dislike the close proximity of another child; they seem alert to possible attack and if touched only slightly are liable to erupt. They are therefore placed well apart to reduce the possibility of provocation by poking and hitting. A particularly undeveloped, dependent child who passively clings and is not involved in the activity at all, is likely to be with one of the adults, while an unrestrained, potentially out-of-control child is close to the other adult, a restraining hand put out when needed. The children least able to follow what is happening, or who are very restless, are usually in the front. Some seem incapable of independent coherent action, but if they appear to want to take part, they are shown individually what to do, and the action is performed with them. The children who make no attachment and do not relate to the group, are left on the sofa with a soft toy; group time in the home area means nothing. They will be passively contained within the structure of the day and will get their individual time later, when they will learn to look at the teacher and make and accept touch.

Making eye contact

The children have been brought together in the carpeted area and have been helped to sit without touching each other. Everything has been taken slowly. The teacher faces them and speaks very quietly and slowly, drawing their attention to the teacher's face as they are named one by one. The child's name comes first, to attract attention, and the request to 'look at me' follows. Eye contact is thus made individually. The children get recognition and approval for this, one by one. They wait, and get approval for waiting. The teacher looks round the group and acknowledges the children and shows pleasure when eye contact is made. The children are repeatedly addressed individually by name and positive comments are made.

Establishing and maintaining eye contact is very important, for in making eye contact, they acknowledge the possibility of a relationship. Attention is therefore given to this from the beginning, and continues whatever the age phase. Quiet insistence brings eye contact in most cases, but the process is very gentle for children who find this distressing. The adults do not intrude with children who are passive and unresponsive, who actively avoid eye contact or avert their gaze or whose eyes wander because they are distractible and cannot involve themselves. Eye contact is encouraged later when one to one with one of the adults who usually makes touch first, tentatively, though this might not be acceptable to some children for a long time. When children are used to this, they might gently take their hands and look at them at eye level. They might blinker them with their hands to encourage eye contact, and gently insist: 'Look at me, look at my eyes.' A big smile of pleasure follows when their eyes meet. Children who are resistive and resentful are more likely to respond at the 'breakfast' table when food is being handed round, or when a situation lends itself to humour, and the first eye contact, albeit indirect, may be when child and adult look at each other in the mirror. The adults continue to direct their attention to what is required, and ask them to look at them; their requests are simple, direct and positive, and if necessary are repeated until the contact is acknowledged. These details are important because few children heed the adults and need this help to be biddable and responsive. They have little sense of personal identity, and so their existence as individuals, and the relationship with the adults that is expected, has to be stressed. Making eye contact is their first achievement, followed later by accepting touch.

Special consideration is given for children who have been brought up in cultures where eye contact with the adult is avoided as a mark of respect or contrition, but practitioners are sensitive to this.

Non-verbal signals

Many of the children pay no attention to the expression on the adult's face or tone of voice, though a few stare fixedly, apprehensively vigilant for any indication that they are doing wrong. These non-verbal signals are initially beyond their experience and mean nothing to them. Often, communication at home is not a mutually adaptive and progressing interaction but is a statement of the parent's caring or control, shown in a caress or a smack, or it reflects their feelings and is not relevant to the child's needs or behaviour. The meaning of these non-verbal signals and their alerting function, the feelings and wishes they indicate and the response expected, is their next learning experience.

So the adults next draw their attention to their faces and voices. They ask them to notice their facial expressions and tone of voice, and link this with their feelings: 'Look at my face' (indicating); 'Look how pleased I am'. Few of the children register their expression so they exaggerate this and many times during the day will say, 'Look at my face', and indicate. In the relaxed peacefulness of the home area, some children for the first time become aware of the adults' faces and expressions, their gestures and tone of voice and what all these mean. Later, when they are more secure and are more aware of themselves and each other, the adults comment on the expression on their faces, and might send them to the mirror to look. The adults interpret their feelings from the expressions on their faces, and develop games centring round the interpretation of facial expressions.

A slow pace and simple language

The children have been helped to make eye contact and to give attention but are likely to have difficulty in maintaining this and following through what is said to them. The adults therefore continue to draw attention to themselves many times, perhaps by doing no more than speaking the child's name, very quietly. They verbalize what they are doing and their expectations. They talk very slowly and deliberately, in short simple sentences, because the children have difficulty in following complex language, and in sustaining attention beyond the first word or two. Everything is taken slowly, for only in this way are the children able to settle, attend and listen. It may take them a long time to settle, but the adults accept this without anxiety because it is an important and essential part of the day and comes before everything else. At first, it is enough for them to sit where required and to give their attention momentarily, and in this calm, quiet and relaxed setting, most of the children do begin to settle, give attention and wait. Later, the requirements are increased, but nothing starts until everyone is quiet and is purposefully attending.

Some of the children remain restless. Others sit passively, are unresponsive and give no attention, or are sullen and resistive. Occasionally, a child hits out at another sitting nearby. The children find it difficult to sit still, but no comment is made and no disapproval is shown. If several are particularly restless, the adult might ask all of them to put their hands in their laps. They are able to give attention to keeping their hands in their laps if told to, otherwise they fidget with them or poke each other. They are able to sit still and concentrate when given a specific detailed instruction. They need to be told exactly what to do.

A concept of group

When all the children are reasonably well settled, the teacher might say, 'Who is here today?' and answers the question by looking at each child in turn and identifying them by name: 'Yes ... is here today. Good.' Then: 'How many children are here today?' When this has been established: 'Who is not here today?', 'How many children are not here today?', 'How many boys are here today? How many girls?', 'How many more boys than girls?'. This interchange draws the children's attention to the others in the group. They notice them and recall their names, and reminders of the ones who are away evoke a memory of what they are like, and sometimes a sense of concern and caring. All this reinforces a sense of group. And incidental to this is an experience of basic number. Each time, the teacher gives back to the children in a short, simple sentence the information elicited. Then their names are written down to affirm their presence in the group. The children continue to wait, their eyes on the teacher. Purposeful waiting is a basic learning experience, and they are able to wait, sit still and give attention because they are given explicit direction. After one or two interested observations, perhaps pleasure at the calm way they came into the classroom, the day's more formal work begins.

One child might now be chosen to count the name cards on the wall chart, from left to right in order, and then go round the group, counting the children. Each child is touched as they are counted; usually this is acceptable because the reason is clear and the contact is anticipated and limited. The teacher asks again:

'How many children are here today?' This leads on to: 'How many drinks/biscuits/pieces of fruit will we need?' They are reminded to add two. This reinforces the sense of group and the adults as part of the group, and they are associated with the satisfaction of the snack to come. Interest is heightened and attention-giving. Once again, they have had an experience of basic number.

Time is structured

The day of the week is established. It is Tuesday and followed on from yesterday, which was Monday. At this point, they might chorus the sequence of days and clap when they come to the right one for 'today', or cards are held up, one by one, showing the days of the week, and the children say when they see the right one for 'today'. 'Yes. Today is Tuesday. What do we do on Tuesdays? We do PE on Tuesdays. Today is Tuesday and we do PE today.' The card showing Tuesday is slotted into the wall chart. Later on, when they are secure in their knowledge of the days of the week, the month would also be recorded, though it might be enough at first to learn that days have names. Friday is given special note because it is the last day of the school week, and the weekend follows, and on Monday they are reminded that Monday is the first day of the school week, and comes after the weekend. These concepts, and the language that denotes them, are built in slowly, one at a time, and are reinforced daily for as long as needed. Even for some older children, it is a novel idea that there is something called a weekend, and that the weekend is different. Many of the children have disorganized lives; basic events are without pattern, and they have no experience of sequence from which to predict. It cannot be assumed that when Friday comes, they know that they do not come to school the next day, and on Monday some may not recall that they did not come to school the day before. For most of them, life is without meaningful form; they have no sense of sequence and pattern, and the way time is structured has to be learned.

An informal chat might follow, about their clothes, the weather or any theme that means something to them and is within their everyday experience. One or two might be eager to give their personal news. Others have nothing to say: they cannot recall what has happened immediately before; their perceptual world barely impinges, experiences are not connected and events go by unrecognized. They are reminded of something they did yesterday and step by step anticipate what is going to happen today: 'We are going to have breakfast again today.' Imagery and expectancy are evoked, and the concept of the 'family breakfast' is consolidated. They are reminded of group procedures, thereby establishing a sense of order and the notion of limits.

Refocusing activities

Action songs, rhymes or drama and dance for older children focus their attention on themselves. It is something they can do that is directly linked to the adults and channels their energy. They ask the children to look at them and to watch. The request is gently repeated and specifically addressed to any child who has not responded. They ask them again to watch what they do and to join in if they can. It might involve no more than the children touching, exploring and naming different parts of their face but the experience makes an important contribution to body awareness and identity. The songs and rhymes can be done loudly/softly and quickly/slowly, and the words that accompany the actions extend their basic vocabulary. Stopping and starting, waiting and taking turns, contribute both to self-control and to a sense of time. The adults speak slowly; their language is simple, every step is specified, and they provide an immediate and visible model.

The children respond to varying extents, some not at all, even though they may have taken part in this activity often in the past. Others watch and try to follow, though might quickly get lost. Others, again, take part with zest and enjoyment. Children who rush in without restraint are likely to need direct help. If necessary, the activity is stopped and when everyone is still, they start again with reminders of what to do. No pressure is put on those who do not take part. Some sit and watch at first, and begin to take part of their own accord by shadowing the others as their confidence grows, or they begin to feel reassured that it is permissible and might even be fun and tentatively join in. Others take no part and will later have time with one adult individually. Those who could take part but refuse are also left till later; children who are only tenuously attached in the group remain by the adult's feet or holding hands. If they wander off, they are followed. One adult stays close by, involving them in a simple activity with physical contact; or keeping an eye on them from a distance, if this seems more appropriate.

Body awareness and identity

This physical outlet in body-centred activities is important. It channels children's restlessness into simple motor activities which are adult-centred and adult-controlled – songs, rhymes, finger and hand games, simple dance steps – and interest most of the children, engage their attention and can be adapted for different ages. They give them intense pleasure and their competence is a source of pride and achievement. These activities are more manageable than giving news which requires recall, verbalization and the ordering of ideas, and presupposes that events were registered at the time. The children are not at the stage of interacting constructively with each other but are able to take part in a simple group activity because they are linked through this to the adults and experience their approval. The activities become part of the basic routine, a class ritual; they are a source of security and well-being and engender a positive sense of group and can be developed into more complex activities requiring more concentration.

If the children remain restless, the adults introduce an activity that is even simpler and more basic, one that will draw them back to an awareness of themselves and will strengthen the links and will settle them: 'Show me your fingers. Touch your nose.' The children are brought back to the security of these simple familiar routines when too much has been expected of them and they have lost their way. These activities have intrinsic importance because they provide the pleasure of the rhythm of the rhyme and the satisfaction of the repetition which contributes to a sense of pattern and organization.

Hand and finger games contribute to an awareness of body and body image and give a sense of identity, physical wholeness and containment and, for some of the children, a sense of their existence as they touch themselves and each other. Many of them seem unaware of their bodies and the relationship of one part to another, and cannot appropriately direct their movements to indicate as required. In these games, the children become aware of their own bodies and their own skin, and establish their body boundaries as they make skin contact with others.

Attachment and trust are being established

In these games in the home area, the children begin to respond to the adults as people, to follow where they lead; they experience satisfaction and well-being in the achievement and in the shared pleasure. Attachment and trust are being established through the achievement and are reinforced by constant repetition.

Touch

For some of the children, the activities are important for establishing physical contact in a way that is acceptable. Many resist touch of any kind and even accidentally brushing against another child sometimes triggers a tantrum. Some who at first hold back want to make physical contact and gradually draw closer and might lean towards the adults and touch them; children who are even more timid begin to draw close and also want to touch them. They become part of the group and begin to tolerate the close proximity of other children. Some are particularly reluctant to make physical contact during the course of these activities. They make no response to a natural and spontaneous overture from the adult, and may resist or reject it, though seem to want it. Some are self-aware and may not want to be noticed making physical contact except during the course of an incidental game. Others are overtly hostile, and resent and reject any form of contact, as they resent and reject a relationship. Most of the children, however, respond to physical affection and the comfort and close physical proximity and intimacy of the home area fosters easy and natural physical contact. The children begin to sit closer together, and build up attachment and trust for each other, as well as for the adults.

Touch is essential for building and maintaining attachment and trust (Gerhardt, 2004). The school's policy must be clear and unambiguous.

Introducing more complex content

All the activities usual in a nursery or KS1 class are later introduced in the home area with variations for older children: feeling objects in a bag and guessing what they are, simple hiding, finding and remembering games. These games are done repeatedly until the children understand what is expected and can join in, however inadequately or tentatively. Variations are introduced with a comment such as 'We will do it this way now', because the children have not sufficient experience, understanding and flexibility to cope at this stage with even a slight change, unless they are told that it *is* a change. The next step is to make the activity or game slightly more formal by building in simple constraints in the form of rules.

Before beginning anything, the adults wait until everyone is sitting as required, without talking. If the game or activity has started and there is any poking or pinching, everything is stopped immediately. Often, it is sufficient for one adult to stop, for many of the children are totally dependent on the support gained from watching and following their actions. Gradually, they are able to manage longer sessions that have more complex content, but if they become restless, the activity is changed to something simpler, or they do something involving gross movement or, if particularly restless, are taken outside to run in the playground.

Structuring the way ahead

The children are now ready to be launched into individual activities. This is more difficult, even for those who will get individual help, because they are no longer linked directly with the adults but indirectly through their toys or equipment, and they are required to do something in relation to these. This is difficult as few of them are able to give attention and persist, predict, anticipate and plan; they may not understand where the teacher's instructions are leading or the practical consequences of even a simple action. Poor tolerance for frustration, and an inability to share and to choose, also limit effective functioning, but direct specific attention to these comes later. At this early stage, they first of all need help in learning how to experience and use the materials, and are not expected to share and choose.

The adults provide support and control

The children are launched into their activities from the home area. This is where personal contact with the adults has been established, and the support and control inherent in this is likely to be maintained when they are no longer close by. Some of the children are not involved in the happenings about them but others are expectant. They are waiting for a lead but nothing happens until everyone is looking and attending. The teacher and assistant also need to be clear about their respective roles, for instance who will take the lead for a particular child.

'Holding'

This is essential for those children who cannot wait but plunge in unheeding, and is a reassurance and support for those who are confused and unventuring, or fearful of failure. Therefore, constraints continue to be built in, and the request might begin with: 'Sit very still. I'm going to tell you what to do. Sit still until I say your name.' In most groups at the beginning of the year, and always when management problems are severe or the children are very unformed, very limited activities are provided; nothing is beyond the child's experience. At this early stage, the teacher might be associated with the toys and equipment in a direct and visible way by handing them to the children one by one. The items thus carry with them the adult's expectations, controls and support, and have enhanced value. Later, when they have more autonomy, they help themselves. This procedure avoids the confusion and overstimulation of making a choice and reduces squabbling. Children who are very inexperienced and insecure are relieved when the adult chooses the activity, or offers a specified and named choice. Instructions are given in detail, to every child individually, spoken quietly, in close physical proximity, with eye contact and touch where appropriate. Everything is taken slowly in simple manageable stages because many of the children grasp only one thing at a time and find it difficult to follow through a simple verbal sequence. All stages of a request or instruction are specified in short, simple sentences, in clear sequence, without ambiguity, because instructions that appear to be simple may involve unfamiliar concepts and be linguistically complex, or may require an understanding of a novel situation. For individual children, the adults pick out the essential features of the activity so that attention is focused. They stress the sequence of events, where this is leading, and give reminders which help them to manage on their own. The slow pace is a brake on the more impetuous children, reassures those who are unforthcoming and provides a sense of orderliness and containment. All activities and explanations are broken down into simple, manageable stages with a great deal of repetition.

Limited choice

Many of the children want everything they see and grab, but then do not know what to do with what they have grabbed, bang or discard it or give up in frustration or have a tantrum. Others see no purpose in the toys and throw them about or kick them. Others roam about, momentarily glancing, briefly touching. A few settle initially but are highly distractible and do not persist. Others are listless and want nothing or are inert and do nothing. They need to have their activities chosen for them and they need direct help from the adults in engaging with them at a very early developmental level. They can do little on their own and the task of the adults, as with parents of babies and toddlers, is to so structure the requirements that they always know what to do, what is expected, and are never left without adequate support. This requires the teacher to have a perceptive awareness of the complexity of the experiences offered in relation to the developmental level of each child, for even a simple activity may involve unexpected difficulty.

Irrespective of their developmental level, many of the children lack personal organization and there are unexpected deficits of experience and understanding even in those who are more advanced. No assumptions are made about the ability of any of them to use the simplest toys and materials without help. They may have attended nursery but have not necessarily engaged with the activities and few, whether secondary or primary age, have the resources to use nursery-level toys and equipment purposefully, or play together constructively. Their level of play is in many cases at the one- or two-year level; they need experiences at this level in learning how to handle basic materials and simple toys.

Learning to choose

In an established group, those children who are familiar with the routine and resources and are sufficiently competent to manage to some extent on their own, are sent off first. They are given a choice only if they have enough experience and maturity; choosing depends on the earlier assimilation of a wide range of experiences and the memory of these experiences and the associated satisfactions. It also requires the discipline to forgo the things that are not chosen, and a sense of purpose. The children sent off next would probably be given a choice from two familiar things. They choose, but their choice is from the teacher's prior choice, and this would be only from activities they know and have fully experienced. If given a completely free choice, almost all would dither or become aimless, and fights might start; or one child might choose the same limited activity over and over again. In time, when they can anticipate the possibilities and satisfactions of activities they do not know, and can predict what these will be, they will have a free choice.

Teacher-directed activities

At this stage of the day, the only toys and activities on offer have inherent structure, are teacher-directed and give opportunity to revisit learning at the Early Years Foundation Stage.

Most of the children are eager to begin. The more competent children are the first to be launched. As they cross the room and set out their things, the others listen to the instructions given, and watch with interest and anticipation. This gives them a shadowy experience of *their* next step forward. They take in the choices available and the adults' comments as they try to help and direct each child, and the choice finally made by the child. Watching what the others do is an important part of the learning experience. Waiting, too, is an important experience, and as they watch, they are likely to build in imagery and savour the experience vicariously in imagery.

Individual support

Eye contact is made with individual children as they go off. This slows them down and helps to maintain the relationship. Clear instructions at this point give direction and an expectation of success, thus providing security as well as implicit control. The support given is individual to the child: their name, a smile, touch. Reassurance to a more capable child is given by the comment, 'I know you can manage on your own' or 'I'll come and help you later'. One adult is there to receive any children who need special help, and at the beginning of the year, all the children get this support. Children who are poorly orientated to their surroundings are taken by the hand and helped into a chair. The children left till last are those who are least able to manage on their own, because they are either too inexperienced or not sufficiently able to control their own behaviour, or both. The teacher chooses a toy or an activity for each of these children and takes opportunities as they arise to acknowledge them when their eyes meet and to make gentle unthreatening contact through touch. For young children, their first full involvement is very basic: rocking and cradling, baby games and nursery rhymes on the adult's knee and a smile may be the child's biggest achievement. Older children may need to have opportunities for this level of involvement built in through creative work or drama.

The structure of the day

- This first session is teacher-controlled and the activities are quiet, individual and contained.
- After this, the children are drawn back to the home area where they are once again helped to settle and attend.

The pattern of the day that follows varies with the timetable of the school and the developmental level of the children but all the groups are based on the same principles and the essential components are the same. The teacher describes step by step the event ahead so that the children are aware of the total experience and are helped to manage the transitions (see Chapter 6).

- In some schools, assembly begins the day, and because it demands considerable self-control is usually followed by a short period of quiet, peaceful, undemanding teacher-centred and teacher-directed group work in the home area.

- KS2 or 3 children, after assembly, might be launched from the home area into structured play or practical activities, chosen and controlled by the teacher. All these activities impose organization on children who have little organization of their own. They provide purpose, give security and are less demanding than undirected free play.
- The breakfast which follows is a relaxation and satisfaction, and a continuing support. Later, the children can manage a period of National Curriculum work and breakfast becomes an acknowledgement of their achievement.
- The teacher brings the children to the carpet, and resettles them with a simple game.
- Playtime comes next (see Chapter 7). They go to the toilet first, in an orderly file, and afterwards wash their hands. They have to be reminded to do this and every stage is treated as a separate operation and has to be demonstrated.

> An assistant: 'If you say "Push up the sleeves of your jumper", a boy wearing a shirt doesn't respond. He thinks it doesn't apply to him, so all relevant clothing has to be specified.'

- After playtime, the children assemble on the carpet and the teacher comments on the way they behaved in the playground. The adults' expectations are reiterated. The children become so used to the ritual that they sometimes say, 'you didn't ask us how we came in'.
- They now work at their appropriate National Curriculum level, possibly sitting in two groups with an adult to each. This will generally be literacy or numeracy focused and will probably include practical work directly related to earlier key stages. Some children may return to their ordinary class for some subjects.
- At the end of the morning, they gather together on the carpet, review the morning's activities, sharing achievements and listening to a story or poem. Arrangements and expectations for lunchtime are rehearsed. They know who will be their midday supervisor and what to do if a difficulty occurs.
- For the afternoon session, they are once again sent off from the

carpet but this time they are free to choose from activities selected by the teacher. When the group is stable, the activities available to the more experienced children involve more movement and encourage cooperation, and extend to role play, sand, water, paint and construction for those who can manage them. The adults are actively involved and take every opportunity to extend the children's language and mathematical concepts as well as creativity and imagination.

* The day ends with a story and a review of what they have done and learned.

Opportunities at the 0–3 year level

It can be difficult at first to gauge the needs of the children and often activities are pitched at too high a developmental level. Many KS1 children and some from KS2 or 3 are not ready for many of the processes involved in creative art work, for instance. Activities at the beginning of EYFS are more appropriate, and some older children will accept and enjoy baby toys if given an appropriate opportunity. For such children, it is useful to consider what would interest a child of two years of age or younger, and provide experiences accordingly, within a consistent routine and through simple games. They are able to give attention and persist at this level; they need the basic perceptual-motor experiences and repetition these provide and get satisfaction from them.

One infant school with an established nurture group adjoined an adventure playground which housed a project for disaffected secondary boys. Some of them would come into the school to play alongside the reception-class children, and especially enjoyed playing with sand and water, building up, knocking down, pouring and splashing. Strong relationships developed. One 15-year-old gave up stealing cars and later went on to train, very successfully, as a driving instructor.

The teacher is alert to extending the learning as opportunities arise. There is a wide developmental range in most groups and some children also need activities linked to later key stages.

Individual help

Each child continues to get individual help for as long as it is needed. The children may need to be taken by the hand and shown what to do because they cannot find out by themselves. At first, they need to watch and join in when they are able to. They need to be played *with*, to do things with the adult, to experience a sense of 'we' 'together' before they can do things on their own. Children only learn by discovery if they have had prior experience of earlier, more elementary discovery, have internalized simple basic concepts, and have a sense of self and purpose that enables them to use and extend these concepts in a new situation. These children have not.

> Some children need to be told that they can touch the toy and hold it, can take the bricks out of the box and be shown and told that the bricks are hard and they can build with them. They need to be shown the right way up to hold the doll, and how to put on the clothes. Those who are poorly coordinated need to be taken by the hand to the toy and shown how to sit on the floor in relation to the toy; some sit with their legs wide apart, as though 18 months old. It is sometimes enough to learn how to open the box and take out the contents, and watch what the teacher does. Other children, who are excited, exuberant and eager for experiences, may well rush in without restraint. They need to be slowed down, to be told to look and listen. The teacher might hold their hands and ask them to look at her: 'No. Look at me. Look at my eyes.' If they stretch out for the toy before she has finished explaining what to do, she holds it in both hands or keeps the lid on the box as she explains, and hands it over only when they are settled and ready. Unless they are 'held' and then 'let go' gradually, they will rush in eagerly and within seconds will be 'aggressive and disruptive'. Other children can pay attention to a wider perceptual field, can grasp what is required and remember what to do. When asked to notice and remember how the bricks are arranged in the box, and to put them back the same way when they have finished, they are able to do this.

Modelling

Before anything new is introduced, the adults always talk about it beforehand and model (DfEE, 1998: 8) what to do.

They might begin by attracting the children's attention with enthusiasm to a simple representational toy which they identify by name. They describe its salient features: 'Look. It's a bus. It's red. It has wheels. Watch', and they develop the action in a simple way with accompanying words, verbalizing what they are doing as they demonstrate what to do, and they register their actions and feelings in language that is basic and is parent–baby/toddler-level in structure and quality. All new activities are introduced gradually and are built up slowly in simple manageable stages. Few of the children know what is expected and they all need the pleasure of a shared activity and the shared feeling that flows from this. This is a developmental need and for as long as is necessary the adults take part in these activities with them. If a child is new to the group, sometimes the adults spend time playing together and gradually involving the child. In this way, new children see constructive interaction between them in a relaxed and happy family atmosphere, can listen to their commentary on what they are doing and what they *see* they are doing, and if hesitant realize that it is permissible for them to try it too. It is important that they see the end result before they try it for themselves, because they may not know what this should be. In a home offering normal opportunities, children see activities taken to completion long before they have the skills to attempt them for themselves.

An attentive presence: 'withitness'

The children engage with the toys and activities because they are appropriate and because expectations are at an earlier, more realistic and relevant level than in the mainstream class. They learn to play and explore with confidence, interest and pleasure because the adults are attentive, fully involved and enjoy these experiences with them and when left to play by themselves, the adults stay nearby. They try to be alert all the time to possible difficulties, to be 'withit' (Kounin, 1970) and intervene with help and encouragement. If they are busy, they let the child know that they will help as soon as they can and the children are repeatedly reminded to ask for help if they are not able to manage. Problems arise because the children's tolerance for frustration is low. They get upset if things go wrong, and most have difficulty in sharing and taking turns. But even when they are familiar with the materials and toys, and can manage to play on their own, they continue to need the support of doing things with the adults. This emotional need for a shared satisfaction may persist for a considerable time. Even more advanced children continue to need a great deal of help and the adults involve themselves as needed, individually with a child or in small groups. They do things with and for them, showing them how to fit things together, how things work, verbalizing all the time, and all the time naming things, feeding in explanations, information, suggestions and ideas, and giving help with basic skills and techniques. They are alert to the complexities of all situations, however simple they appear to be. Difficulties, however trivial they may seem, are anticipated, and the children are told what to expect and with this extra help are usually able to develop their activities.

Communication and language

Verbal reinforcement and elaboration is very important for early language development; in the nurture group, it is conveyed mainly through a running commentary to a greater extent than there would be in the normally supportive home because the children must catch up quickly. The adults describe and explain, and with the more advanced children, discussion and patient reasoning are possible. They voice their thoughts as they talk together, as though thinking aloud. They verbalize the nature of difficult situations, how people feel and behave, and they comment and share observations. This 'lesson' gives the children an experience of the way people think, how they reflect on what they are doing and how they work things out (see Chapter 6).

Persistence and repetition

Young children who are developing normally engage totally with an activity that is at the appropriate level and of their own accord persist with it and repeat the experience. (Goldschmied,

1987; Goldschmied and Jackson, 2004) but most nurture children cannot persist. In the nurture group, they are expected to persist with an activity for as long as the adults require. The adults' expectations are realistic and they might provide support by showing them on the clock how much longer they have to go or provide something else only when it is clear that they have reached the limits of their persistence. The children do not change of their own accord because they would not settle any better but would flit from one thing to another or grab at the first thing that attracts their attention. The adults' insistence that they persist averts aimless and unproductive behaviour. Although the children may resist at first, they accept this requirement, and when restricted in this way, become absorbed in their activity and seem very satisfied. Because the pace is slow, and there is a lot of repetition, there is time for the experience to be consolidated and internalized. Later, when given a choice of activity, the children often return to these same simple things repeatedly as young children do at home. It is important to allow the children to return to these simple activities and re-experience them. They recapture the basic satisfaction and security they gained through this early play, and have the comfort of assured success.

Not all the children are at a baby/toddler level. Some come into school with a more adequate experience and are able to use materials and toys that are more advanced and have greater flexibility and imaginative potential. If they are able to choose their activity, the adults try to ensure that it is within their capacity and attention span, and can be finished in a reasonable time, and that they will be able to tolerate any interference from a child nearby. They, too, are expected to persist with their activity and see it through to completion, and if they want to change they must have a good reason. One of their difficulties is dissatisfaction and restlessness, not settling and persisting, repeatedly seeking they know not what. Quietly setting limits helps to contain their restlessness and eventually leads to sustained interest in the task. Those children who have more autonomy are able to initiate change for themselves, but *all have to ask* if they want to start anything new.

Protected play space

In the early days, the adults control and supervise each child's play space. Few of them can interact constructively with other children or even play alongside each other without interfering, whether by intent or accident. They need to play alone in their own unimpeded play space and situations where space has to be shared are avoided.

Sharing

At this stage, the children are not expected to share equipment. They need their own things, usually chosen by the adult, and if they grab or fight, the toy is taken away. They might pout, sulk or have a tantrum, but their resentment is short-lived and very soon they accept something else. They need to play repetitively and alone at a very simple level. With this help, many of them quickly become engrossed in their activities and are increasingly able to sustain their attention. Later, they are able to share space, materials and toys, and cooperate with another child. Later still, the adults carefully control and monitor an activity involving the physical participation of two or more children. Cooperative work is possible only when the children are able to acknowledge each other, however minimally, and with reminders can tolerate the frustration of holding back, waiting, sharing and giving way for others sufficiently well to keep the activity intact. As the children achieve greater competence, individual and class activities become more complex.

Experiencing achievement

When the children are 'held' within the organization and structure of the nurture group day, the adults are free to tune in to individual children, and respond to and acknowledge in a developmentally appropriate way any small feature of behaviour that is in a forward-moving direction.

For children who are unresponsive and barely function, the aim of the adult would be to elicit a smile and encourage the slightest sign of initiative. Their first achievement might be to empty a box of bricks of their own accord, and the warmth and pleasure of the adult's spontaneous and immediate appreciation, expressed in a hug or huge smile, tells them that it is permissible to do this. If they build a tower, they might need 'permission' to knock it down, and the adult may have to knock it down first to reassure them that this really is permissible and 'safe'. They have the shared pleasure of the daring and the noise, and the children sense approval for having done it. Making a noise, daring to exist, is their achievement. For more advanced children, being quiet when this is required might be the achievement, and the adult's approval would be more muted, perhaps no more than 'well done' and for some children, a smile of satisfaction.

Achieving, consolidating and extending learning

The adults respond intuitively to the children's achievements, but it is vital that they formulate their needs in order to provide a situation which enables them to achieve. These small steps towards progress in the developmental strands are targets for their Individual Education or Behaviour Support Plans (IEP or BSPs). Observations made during group times enable the adults to notice how the children respond, their mood, what they can and cannot do and where further help is needed. This is also a useful time to comment on their achievements and progress.

It is important that each forward step taken is acknowledged and also consolidated; when to re-experience an earlier stage, when to consolidate current learning and when to move forward may be particularly difficult issues in the case of academically able children. A single situation can, however, yield different kinds and levels of experience. For instance, playing in the sand may be extended into weighing and measuring and also provide a much needed basic perceptual experience. Experienced practitioners know that experiences are multi-dimensional and different kinds of learning go on simultaneously, though they are watchful not to expect too much and resist the temptation to move the children on too quickly. It is a relief to think of the children as two years of age or thereabouts, for the adults can then relax, reassured to feel that their behaviour is 'normal', and that National Curriculum achievements are not the immediate priority. Finding the right balance is vital. The children settle into the routine of the day and when they are calm and with the demands of the mainstream class in mind, it is tempting to move them on too quickly, but if they do, the situation could fall apart. The quiet, peaceful, slow-moving periods of the nurture group day are for consolidation. This is the time when the adults relax quietly together, just as they would at home. The children like the feeling that the teacher and assistant are sitting quietly together and if the adults sit still, they sit still. They seem to be taking in the attachment, the peace and the security and a sense that all is well.

Ensuring success

For the children to experience achievement, the organization of the nurture group day must provide maximal opportunities for success and must ensure that the adults are relaxed enough to notice and acknowledge the success. They must be alert all the time and aware of the complexities of all situations, however simple they seem, and break them down into manageable stages. The children's success is evident and is reinforced by the response of the adults who share in it. This is immediate and appropriate for the achievement concerned, whether a hug, or a touch on the shoulder with an exclamation of pleasure or simply a satisfied, supportive, verbal comment.

Nurture groups work well when the adults are attentive to the many points of detail. This sounds daunting but, as with families, it is the underlying attitude and general trend that is important. Teachers or assistants new to the work absorb the 'flavour' of the nurture groups and then get on with it in their own personal and spontaneous way. Losing some points of detail does not matter – it happens in all families – but if too many are lost, the group will not provide a nurturing experience for the children. They need to be 'good enough' (Winnicott, 1960). What must be absorbed above all is the early level at which most of the children function. 'Think of them as two; that's all you need to do.'

Summary ☐

- Behaviour is understood as communication: close observation and assessment using the Boxall Profile is the starting point for intervention.

- Children and young people in nurture groups, whatever their age, have an underlying need for attachment and early learning experiences.

- Manageable routines and security are the context for learning to attend in a group.

- When experiences are at the appropriate developmental level and are carefully structured, children begin to achieve.

Further reading

Bennathan, M. and Boxall, M. (1998) *The Boxall Profile Handbook: A Guide to Effective Intervention in the Education of Pupils with Social, Emotional and Behavioural Difficulties.* London: Nurture Group Network. This is essential reading *before* using the Boxall Profile for assessment.

Some of the basic texts on pedagogy can usefully be re-read with nurture children of different ages in mind, particularly:

Katz, L.G. (1998) *A Developmental Approach to the Curriculum in the Early Years.*

Kounin, J. (1970) *Discipline and Group Management in Classrooms.* New York: Holt, Rinehart and Winston. Both this and the text above can be found in Pollard, A. (ed.) (2002) *Readings for Reflective Teaching.* London: Continuum.

Laird, G. (2009) 'Babies help boys reach new maturity', *Times Educational Supplement* 20, February. Initiatives such as Baby Matterz suggest possibilities for nurture work at KS3 and 4.

Lucas, S., Insley, K. and Buckland, G. (2006) *Nurture Group Principles and Curriculum Guidelines: Helping Children to Achieve.* London: Nurture Group Network. The discovery basket described here helps brain development; children and young people learn to persist and concentrate.

4

The Internalization of Controls

This chapter describes how nurture group practitioners:

- structure and organize the children's day, meeting their needs for emotional security and helping them make constructive relationships
- have clear guidelines to give children a sense of direction and purpose
- make their roles and expectations clear
- recognize that acceptable behaviour has to be learnt; that control is internalized through consistent management and attention to detail.

Most nurture group children initially have no understanding of the teacher's role. They do not heed the teacher but behave as they will, without direction and forward-moving purpose, unable to engage constructively in events about them. Some are without basic competencies and social skills, and inadvertently and unwittingly cause disturbance. Others are unhappy and fractious, resistive and rejecting, and are destructive in their hurt and anger. Others, again, have internalized negative attitudes and are destructive and disruptive in intent; they get relief from hurting and depriving others, and for some this is a satisfying pleasure. In many children, primitive fear is readily aroused in normally unthreatening circumstances and they become aggressive and difficult to manage. The children's difficulties vary greatly in nature and severity; their behaviour is often described as 'destructive, disruptive and aggressive'. All are symptoms of frustrated purposeful growth. In so far as the task of the nurture practitioners is to promote normal growth, every aspect of their work contributes directly and indirectly to the alleviation of behavioural difficulties.

Normal development is based on a trusting attachment (Robinson, 2003) but this is rarely made immediately and the child's behaviour may negate attachment. The adults' first objective, therefore, is for acceptable behaviour; they impose their requirements and control leads to attachment, trust and the assimilation of constructive learning. The Developmental Strands (second cluster) of the Boxall Profile are the starting point by which they enable the children, whatever their age, to:

• become emotionally secure
• be biddable and able to accept constraints
• be able to accommodate others
• respond constructively to others
• maintain internalized standards.

The process is reinforcing and cumulative. It begins with a relevant structure and organization.

Structure and organization

The organization of the nurture group day has to be the first consideration when establishing acceptable behaviour; the tempo, structure and the clear guidelines are at an early developmental level. Experiences and events are carefully monitored and controlled. This is a major factor in the improved functioning of all the children and in some the change is immediate and dramatic; they understand what is required, the expectations are within their competence and they get direct support and help when needed. They function more effectively, and energy, which is otherwise aimless and undirected, finds appropriate, constructive, satisfying and legitimate outlets. They feel secure, gain satisfaction and experience success and approval. Stress, frustration and provocation for and by all the children are reduced, and fights, tantrums and aggressive attacks on others are less likely to occur.

The level of organization is crucial

Improvement comes about initially because the day is organized for a developmental level where little or no autonomy is expected.

This is of crucial importance. The organization and conduct of the day must be questioned if children's behaviour is still difficult to manage after the settling-in period or they are fractious or having tantrums.

In some groups, the constraints and self-control needed for successful participation in school are built in, as in a family, in a natural and unobtrusive way, and the adults are then mainly concerned with widening children's experience. Many who respond quickly are unventuring and fearful, disorganized and without trust, and their tantrums and fractious behaviour in the mainstream class seem largely a protest, and an expression of their unhappiness, aimlessness and stress. Some of the others need more direct and evident control, but they too settle in quickly. Robust children may be eager for experiences but unable to use them; they plunge into situations beyond their competence and become excited and out of control. They are not purposefully aggressive and disruptive but indirectly cause fights and upsets, mainly because they grab at everything in sight and disrupt and provoke the others. They, too, function better when their experiences are monitored and their behaviour is controlled. The aggression in some other children is more deliberate, and ranges from a sly physical jab at another child to vicious sustained attacks. This may be an expression of unhappiness, anxiety, fear and frustration, or the tension of energy that has no purposeful outlet.

The approach is nevertheless much the same, and differs only in emphasis. Support, care and consistent management are within an ordered day. Strict limits are set, developmentally appropriate outlets are provided and the children are helped to gain legitimate satisfactions at their level of need and competence. Their energy is thus directed more purposefully, their behaviour is more acceptable from the beginning and any difficulties arising are more manageable. Food for these children expresses caring, and treats are a shared satisfaction and pleasure.

Limited opportunities at first

It is important that the experiences available are very limited at first, with little or no choice, and no more available than is necessary for all to be purposefully occupied. Toys and activities are carefully managed, and the more difficult things are out of sight and reach of the less experienced children. The environment is orderly and organized, rules are clear and frequently repeated, the children are under constraints and are carefully let go into their activities. Many of them are without the resources or lack the organization to use a complex environment. They are easily distracted and want everything they see, and unless the situation is strictly controlled, they alight on things at random and use nothing effectively.

Consistency within routine leads to security and trust

The consistency of everyday experiences within a broad routine enables the children to function in an organized and purposeful way, and eventually to predict. The routine is manageable and familiar. It contributes to a sense of trust and, after an upset, provides comfort and reassurance. And because the routines are constraining, they slow the children down, give them time to become aware of themselves in relation to others and the implicit standards that have to be met, and lead to a sense of group identity. All the group activities are important, but the most important are the routines and rituals around food which give comfort and reassurance.

Within the structure provided by routine and organization is a complex web of experiences that builds up trust and a sense of the adults' caring, and leads to attachment and a wish to please. Discussion of feelings and behaviour becomes relevant, and through this the children gradually learn to regulate their own behaviour better and deal more constructively with their feelings of aggression. The role model provided by the adults is crucial. The children are aware of them and begin to behave as they do, and the adults therefore make explicit the constructive and supportive nature of their relationship (Insley and Lucas, 2009).

The essential dependency of the children is nevertheless usually apparent from the beginning; attachment and response in all but a few is established fairly quickly and in the younger children is sometimes striking. Accompanying this is an improvement in the children's behaviour, usually within the first three weeks in a typically developing group, and both adults and children are reassured that all will be well.

Although behaviour quickly becomes manageable when there is clear structure and control, fundamental and lasting change comes about only over time as different facets of the learning experience begin to reinforce each other. The process is cumulative and the learning content becomes part of the child's being. The teacher's requirements have now been internalized, and the child's behaviour is self-directing.

Learning behaviour: general guidelines

Even when the nurture group day is modified appropriately for an early developmental level, aggressive, destructive and disruptive behaviour may nevertheless be the dominant problem for the adults and a worrying feature in the early stages. It nullifies everything they are trying to do, negates potential attachment and disturbs any group feeling that is developing. Each child's difficulties preclude the possibility of their progress as well as that of others who are likely to be provoked and an initially benign situation can rapidly deteriorate. Learning appropriate behaviour is *the* urgent priority and control is strict and unremitting at all times. It demands constant vigilance on the part of the adults and is not at first an intuitive response within a relationship of trust, for effectively there is no relationship, and no trust. It derives from the strength of the adults' conviction that learning to meet basic social demands is a crucial stage in the child's personal growth, and from the strength of the knowledge that adult and child must endure a painful present for a more constructive and fulfilling future. It is through the adults' unremitting direction, and the consistency and immediacy of their response, within a context of fairness and caring, that the children learn to trust, and become attached, dependent and biddable. They are responsive to the adults' responsiveness to them and begin to internalize the security and controls. An assistant in a very difficult group of year 3 and 4 children commented: 'They are all soft inside, really.'

Behaviour problems may be severe

The impact of behaviour problems on the adults can be very great. Particularly in groups of older children when frustration, irritability, tension, anger and fear are at a high level, they readily absorb each others' anxiety and aggression, and powerful, formless feelings break through their fragile controls. Teachers complain that the group is 'high', 'on the boil'. Any teacher control or self-control is lost, aggression rises and behaviour becomes destructive and disruptive. Fights or temper tantrums break out, and even when the group seems stable, it sometimes erupts because one child looks at another. When a situation disintegrates in this way, there is no possibility of the adults exercising control. Normal classroom management strategies are of no avail as there is no relationship between adult and child, no acknowledgement of the existence of the adult, and any interaction between the children is negative. There is no sense of a group, and there can be no appeals to standards, even were the children to listen, because there are no shared values; and there is no response to the adults' feelings because there is no shared experience of feelings.

> The beginning of the morning, particularly on Mondays, is a high-risk period. A small 'breakfast' at about ten o'clock is dramatically stabilizing. The children's attention is held by the food, and the teacher for the first time may be in control. Food at this stage, in groups like this, is not initially an expression of caring. It is a way of indicating the teacher's requirements, and is an agent of control.

It is particularly important that the situation is geared at an appropriate developmental level and that there is meticulous control of the children's experiences. Everything, therefore, is 'writ large'. The tempo is slower, even if the children are older, there is direct support from the moment they arrive at school, and individual help is given as needed. The limits set are very tight and are specified in detail, step by step. The essentials of what is required are made evident and are highlighted, and everything is repeated as often as is necessary.

The adults have clear roles and expectations

The adults make their expectations and attitude quite clear, and their disapproval is immediate. This ensures that the children are successful and reduces the unnecessary frustration and provocation from others that lead to tantrums and fights.

In the early stages of a difficult group, it is helpful to direct the attention of the children exclusively to the teacher, for it is s/he who sets the general style of discipline and the expectations to be met. The assistant supports the children in responding to the teacher's requirements. If both take initiatives at this early stage, the children are likely to be distracted and confused.

Within the framework established by the teacher, both adults are meticulously consistent in their management. They have the same standards where basic behaviour is concerned, and reinforce each other's expectations in their individual ways. They make their attitude to the children's behaviour evident. They show their pleasure clearly, and say 'no' with implacable importance. In saying 'no', the adults might hold a child's hands and purposefully make eye contact as they speak and clap their hands before speaking, if necessary.

The most basic behaviour first

Initially, attention is directed to one feature only of unacceptable behaviour; the developmentally more basic behaviour is tackled first. Swearing is ignored if the children are still physically attacking each other, because it is difficult enough for them to control their fighting, and swearing is an outlet for their aggression. Later, they are helped to say what is wrong, but as they learn to involve themselves in a more constructive and satisfying way, they become less prone to yelling aggressively at each other, and to swearing. Similarly, not grabbing the biscuits comes before not taking the biggest and the best. Later, they can be helped to share and courtesies and a polite manner are then encouraged.

Intervening early

A high level of vigilance and alert response is required of the adults. The principles of classroom management from the Elton

Report (DES,1989: 71) are a familiar part of a teacher's repertoire but in the nurture group they are used within the context of a close parent–child relationship at an earlier developmental level. Thus, scanning and 'withitness' ensure that when the children are not able to cope with their activities or relationships, the need for help is anticipated. Incidental help when the child meets difficulties removes an obstacle to progress; it dispels the anger and frustration of not being able to achieve, and turns a potentially dangerous mood into interest and goodwill, or prevents a sullen mood turning to aggression. Holding children's hands when they are required to wait provides any needed extra support. Deflecting them from what it seems they *might* be going to do, or by saying what the adult's expectations are in advance of their actions, not only defuses a situation but also structures the way ahead, and children usually fall in with this even if it was not their intention. Some of the children are not aware that they have been deflected in this way; others appear to get satisfaction from the realization that they are behaving as required. (See Chapter 5 for the management of temper tantrums and fights.)

The home area: peace and quiet are re-established

If tempers and fights still arise or if the group is becoming disturbed and disorganized, all activities are stopped. The children are drawn into the home area, where they sit down, and the adults wait quietly until they are calm and still. The children are used to being brought back to the home area many times during the day, and at times of stress one adult introduces a simple ritualized activity, perhaps a familiar action song that was learned when they were relaxed, and which they associate with quietness and well-being. Before being let go again, they are given a patient reminder of what to do when difficulties arise. Parents of young children pick them up if they are crawling or toddling into a potentially destructive situation, and hold them close before letting them go and *putting* them somewhere else. The equivalent in the nurture group is for the adults to draw the children to them in the home area, if possible before problems arise, and wait for calm, before letting them go and directing them to something else. Small children are able to explore because they have within them the comfort and security of being nursed and protected in their parents' arms, and are aware of their presence close by. Correspondingly, the home area in the nurture room is established as a quiet place of well-being and security, where good things happen.

Disruptive behaviour: grabbing

Close observation reveals that the aggressive and disruptive behaviour shown by the children, which often seems unprovoked, is rarely so. In the carefully monitored situation of the nurture group, it is often seen to be the consequence, directly or indirectly, of uninhibited grabbing. In the simplest case, the child is attracted to something at a perceptual level, recklessly plunges in and grabs.

> A nine-year-old boy, described as aggressive and disruptive, wrought havoc in the dining hall when he grabbed at a shiny knife; most of the cutlery was dull in finish but a few of the knives were shiny. He wanted the shiny knife, and he grabbed.
>
> A fight broke out between two five-year-olds, a boy and a girl, over some large brightly painted threaded beads. Both wanted them to wear around their necks and they pulled, kicked, bit and screamed until separated. Two adults were needed to calm them, each holding a child.

Such children seem like toddlers who are dominated by perceptual impulse and want all the attractive things they see. They grab, and in their excitement are aware only of the thing they grab. The situation disintegrates as excitement and anxiety rise. Excitement and anxiety turn to aggression. Unproductive behaviour escalates, the first one grabs and the offended child clings on in a fury, and may become further inflamed because this is experienced as an attack and a violation of personal space. Some children are attracted indiscriminately to all the things they see, though frequently settle to nothing. Others seem to have an insatiable need to grab everything, though some seem mainly concerned to deprive the others. Most of them guard what they have, fearing the depredations of others.

Unrestrained grabbing, which has the appearance of greed, is a theme in many of the groups, but the way it manifests itself suggests that the nature and extent of the underlying need varies greatly. It seems to be most marked in those children who have missed out on both experiences and constructive behaviour management, and characteristically these are the most aggressive children. It was particularly evident in the first KS2 group.

Left to themselves, the children grabbed at everything to hand, not only food, and pushed and fought to get at the straws and milk, elbows jabbing and hands outstretched. They grabbed at a biscuit and with biscuit in mouth, they grabbed for another. They grabbed at a jigsaw, a toy car or a crayon. They fought to open the door, or for the coat peg they wanted, they grabbed for something another child had, even if they did not want it or even know what it was, and would force open a tightly clenched fist to take it. They were greedy to be the first and have the advantage, greedy for the biggest and the best, greedy for the brightest and the shiniest. They were greedy for praise, to be acknowledged, to be the best, to be the most favoured, to be the most wanted; and greedy for attention and affection. They were greedy, too, in conversation. Each talked louder than the others and all of them were shouted down. During the first few weeks, the assistant spontaneously described the 'aggressive' children as the 'greedy, grabbing' ones, and the 'withdrawn' children, who were not able to take anything and got left out, as the 'quiet, clinging, homey ones'. In her words: 'The quiet, clinging, homey ones don't grab but keep things to themselves and won't share; the greedy, grabbing children won't share, either.'

The origin of explosive outbursts, otherwise, usually lies in the total involvement of the children with their own immediate interests and anger when thwarted or provoked.

Making the situation manageable

Many of the children are big and strong and can do damage and the adults avoid situations which make demands beyond their level of competence, as with a younger child at home. If they cannot sit close together without digging their elbows into each other and pushing for more space, they are kept apart. If fights start because they grab at a jar full of crayons, they are given one crayon each, and if they want another colour, they have to ask. Everything available is developmentally appropriate, is restricted in scope, and is provided in manageable stages. A new toy is held back if anyone grabs. Children who are unwilling to take what is offered, or pay only scant attention to it, are given nothing else, and the cry 'I want … ' is ignored. Impulsive behaviour, frustration and conflict are in this way controlled.

Teaching social skills

The children who hold back are praised, for with few exceptions, the children want to be the best and get the most praise. The children are taught to ask for what they want and the form in which the request should be made. If the child asks properly, the adult responds immediately; otherwise, *they* make the request and wait for the child to echo it. If the child continues to demand, challenge and swear, they appear not to hear, and make no response. The children seem to experience this social training as a lesson and are eager to succeed and to please. Quickly, they begin to see a connection between the requirements of the adult and the satisfaction of their needs, and the sense of well-being that constructive interaction brings.

Food is a vehicle for basic learning experiences

Some groups are dominated by children who are particularly aggressive and negative. They seem unmanageable and the provision of food is of crucial importance. It gives the adults an opportunity to build in acceptable controls and is particularly important in the early days. For nearly all of the children, food is of primary interest, though is not initially the valued expression of a satisfying relationship. It is something they want and at first may be the only thing to which they give attention, the first time that eye contact is established, and the only situation where they are motivated to wait, and can be helped to wait. Heightened attention is concentrated on the food as they wait, and thus on the adults who they see as giving people. They see themselves in relation to the giving person, begin to get a sense of being attached and valued and learn to acknowledge the adults and develop an expectation of supportive, caring and consistent authority.

'Breakfast'

In groups that are dominated by very difficult 'aggressive and disruptive' children, it is particularly important to provide a 'family' breakfast in addition to that provided by a breakfast club. Typically, these children grab and use destructively anything in sight. Some seem dazzled by the riches of school and take indiscriminately. Others seem to be at a pre-social stage of instant gratification, while others again seem driven by infantile greed. A few are more purposefully destructive and are calculatingly anti-social. Whatever the origin of children's grabbing, it is in many cases an important factor underlying their aggression, or behaviour which seems like aggression, and a 'family' breakfast in school provides the adults with a basic and powerful situation for modifying this behaviour. Breakfast may be no more than a biscuit or a piece of toast and jam, and a glass of milk or juice. But whatever the nature of the food, the situation is a very simple one at first, every detail is carefully monitored and controls are built in stage by stage.

The case study below is from the first KS2 group established; it included nine- and ten-year-olds. A high proportion of the children had serious behaviour problems: they were not biddable, readily attacked each other and some were big enough to be dangerous.

For breakfast at the beginning of the year, everyone had exactly the same food and the same amount, and there was no surplus. The children waited at the table without touching anything while the assistant went to the cupboard. They waited while she took the biscuits from the cupboard, and while she counted them onto a plate; they waited while she put the plate onto a tray and returned to the table. And they watched her and what she did as they waited. When the children were quiet, the assistant said, 'You can take your milk now'. The biscuits were then offered to each child in turn, and each child in turn took one. If any

(Continued)

(Continued)

child was unable to accept this minimal requirement to sit down and be part of the group, he was allowed to have his milk in his own way and to wander about or sit in the corner, but he did not get a biscuit. When this happened, the child concerned sulked. If the children generally were unsettled, even when this was because two or three children were paying no attention, no one was given a biscuit with their milk. The response was usually resentment, or a stunned silence, but the children accepted the teacher's conditions. These same children, when they took a picnic to the park early in the first term, 'grabbed everything that was going, and even when their mouths were stuffed with food still grabbed and wanted more'. On a later expedition to the park, no one was allowed to take a second sandwich until the slowest child had eaten the first. They ate much more slowly and some of the children refused a second sandwich.

Breakfast is faded out

Breakfast is an important feature in the early days, and although conducted in a controlled and purposeful way, the 'strictness' is rarely apparent. This is largely because of the relaxed attitude of the adults, and an approach to the children that is sometimes spiced with humour. Breakfast does not necessarily continue indefinitely; if most of the children are able to conform to basic social requirements, the time is used for other learning.

Reinforcement of waiting is then made over a snack or piece of fruit in the home area, or when the children are playing. A difficulty arises when only one or two children have a serious problem of grabbing at the food, but whether a 'family' breakfast or snack in the home area, the procedure is much the same. Children who cannot tolerate waiting are the first to be given their milk already poured out and are allowed to drink it straight away. When the milk has been drunk and everyone is ready, they are the first to be offered a biscuit, but are required to hold back, albeit momentarily, before taking the biscuit, and the demands are gradually built up as they become increasingly able to cope.

The following more detailed account concerns a child with

severe behaviour problems who was admitted at the beginning of the spring term to a well functioning KS1 group. Breakfast had been discontinued.

At milk and biscuits time, John was the first to be offered a biscuit, because waiting even for the second turn would have been intolerable. When offered the first biscuit, he was required to hold back, however momentarily, before taking it. He quickly learned to wait, and the pleasure of the adults was evident. However, as soon as he had been given a biscuit, he did as he pleased. A second biscuit was therefore handed round the group, and he did not get one. In this way, the teacher demonstrated her requirements. He reacted with shock. At first, he had tantrums and stamped his feet, but quickly conformed. The first biscuit was never withdrawn but he sometimes had it later on his own, and the teacher explained that when he could take his turn, as she required, he could have it with the others. In practice, he rarely had his biscuit later because he could manage to sit still for a moment, and the teacher's expectations were increased only gradually as he became better able to wait. Whatever her requirement, whether waiting for food or persisting with his work, a low level of achievement was accepted at first, but her expectations gradually increased, and each achievement was cherished. The teacher never insisted unless she felt he could achieve, but if she felt he could achieve, she insisted. His experience and self-control, and her insistence, built up together. She was unyielding when she judged her demands to be within his tolerance for frustration and stress. And she always verbalized her expectations and her pleasure in the achievement.

John was being helped individually from the beginning. The caring, constructive nature of the relationship is like that of parents who are sensitively in touch with the pressures the child can tolerate, and yield or resist as they sense whether at that moment he is able to take responsibility for his own behaviour.

Helping the children to learn to wait and not grab requires delicate judgement on the part of the adults. Although they build up their expectations gradually in small manageable stages, the procedure is not dragged out unnaturally because the situation would then be contrived and impersonal, and the children would become frustrated and negative.

Meeting individual needs

Modification of the total situation is the teacher's first task but if real and rapid progress is to be made, the adults must be aware of each child's particular needs, and must be able to meet them. Awareness and involvement, sympathy and interest are the heart of their work. They identify with the child's feelings and work together to understand the difficulties and work on them, each reinforcing what the other says and does. They are alert to notice and acknowledge each small gain, and they try to be consistent in giving immediate recognition, directly related to the behaviour concerned and characterized by clearly demonstrated pleasure.

The adults acknowledge and comment when a child meets their expectations and their pleasure communicates that it matters. They frequently refer to the achievements of the group or particular children and recall what they have done well. Even when an aspect of behaviour has become satisfactorily established, they specifically refer to it from time to time, perhaps in the home area or at the breakfast table, or when there is a feeling of well-being in the group.

Reinforcement

Throughout the day, the adults take every opportunity to make clear their expectations. Repeatedly, they say what is permissible and what is required, and frequently ask the children to repeat back to them. They use to the full every problem arising to demonstrate a social point. They constantly stress desirable behaviour and give simple explanations, reinforced by demonstration and role play when necessary and appropriate. They help the children to see a connection between the requirements that are being stressed and the personal and social consequences, and show them a more constructive way of behaving. Constantly, the adults make clear to each child the needs and feelings of the others and they highlight in their relationship with each other the awareness and consideration for others they are trying to develop in the children. They convey that they value this behaviour and the attitudes that underlie it, and in their insistence that the children meet these standards, they, by implication, value the children and acknowledge them as potentially well-functioning members of the social group.

Satisfying basic needs

Grabbing and keeping and not being able to share are closely linked with 'not having', but in the nurture group the children get the things they want and need: affection, attention, caring physical contact, early basic experiences and the reassurance that they are valued. They get them in manageable amounts and have time to assimilate them and be satisfied by them, and as these needs are increasingly met, they become more able to share. The children have a keen sense of fairness at this stage but they learn that there is enough for everyone and that the adults are fair. They begin to understand the nature of group interaction and that certain standards have general application and validity, are universal social demands and must be maintained. They quickly begin to accept the consequences of bad behaviour, and understand and help to maintain the standards that are being established. They take over the adults' attitudes and make clear to the others what is required, even using their words and tone of voice.

Internalizing standards

At first, the children conform to these basic requirements only because of the adults' control. Later, these standards become more genuinely their own because of their close relationship with the adults, and their consistent experience of being cared for, and the sense of well-being and purpose that comes from constructive relationships with other children. As affections develop between the children, they begin to show concern for each other and to share. They become increasingly secure and satisfied and accept that the other children must have affection and attention from the adults and are able to share this.

The timid, inhibited children, and those who are 'frozen', gain security from the clearly defined structure, seem reassured by the firm and strict control, and begin to see what is acceptable. At first, they hold back and are liable to get left out, but as they experience the care and support of the adults, and the encouragement that follows any initiative they show, they become less fearful and begin to take, and may even begin to grab. Gradually, they, too, learn to share.

Control is constructive

Firm control of behaviour at the beginning is constructive and caring for all the children, irrespective of the nature of their difficulties, and is the essential first step. Within three weeks or so, the children are usually orderly and are able to wait for their turn, though continuing attention to learning behaviour may be needed for a considerable time especially with older children. As behaviour in the group improves, they become more trusting and are less possessive with their things. They know that the adults will ensure that they get a fair share and so they give up for others when this is required or share of their own accord. Without intervention, the children neither use their opportunities constructively, nor experience the satisfaction of the companionship of others.

Summary ☐

- The nurture practitioner's first objective is acceptable behaviour; control comes first, leading to attachment, trust and self-directing behaviour later.
- The child's day is organized for a developmental level where little or no autonomy is expected at first.
- Opportunities are limited and activities and resources are introduced gradually.
- Food, and the accompanying rituals, is an important vehicle for learning behaviour.
- Control is constructive; all children benefit, whatever their difficulty.

Further reading

Docker-Drysdale, B. (1990) *The Provision of Primary Experience: Winnicottian Work with Children and Adolescents.* London: Free Association Books. This book describes the importance of food for children with behavioural difficulties.

Dowling, M. (2002) *Young Children's Personal, Social and Emotional Development.* London: Paul Chapman Publishing. This text has many everyday examples of sensitive early years practice.

Insley, K. and Lucas, S. (2009) 'Making the most of the relationship between two adults to impact on early childhood pedagogy: raising standards and narrowing the attainment gap', in T. Papatheodorou and J. Moyles (eds) *Learning Together in the Early Years.* London: Routledge. Experienced nurture practitioners recognize that the quality of their adult–adult relationship has value in enhancing children's learning. As yet, there is little other literature available.

SEAL resources can be found at www.nationalstrategies.standards.dcsf.gov.uk These are aimed at a later developmental stage than most nurture children but may be useful for older children or for whole-school use.

5

Disruptive Behaviour: Nature and Management

This chapter shows how nurture practitioners:

- are alert to potential difficulties and avoid confrontation whenever possible
- understand the causes of temper tantrums and how careful management leads to a closer relationship
- ensure that other children know what to do if a temper tantrum or fight breaks out
- operate within school policies and procedures for managing tantrums and fights, including restraint, if necessary.

The previous two chapters described how behaviour is learned through the organization and structure of the nurture group following the normal developmental process. Some children's behaviour is more complex. Difficulties which are more deep-seated and sometimes require further intervention (see Chapter 10) are identified in Section 2 of the Boxall Profile: Diagnostic Profile (Bennathan and Boxall, 1998). These children will still make significant gains in the nurture group (Cooper and Whitebread, 2007). Behaviour difficulties of the kind described were a major consideration when the first groups were established.

Observed behaviour

An upsurge of uncontrolled feelings characterizes temper tantrums but they vary greatly in the extent to which control is lost. Some outbursts are little more than an immature expression of distress or anger, in others the child is not in control of himself, may be out of control and is sometimes described as 'going berserk'. Fights, too, are an expression of uncontrolled feelings, but whereas tantrums have a quality of impotence and distress, fights are more consciously purposeful. The child remains organized and relieves feelings of anger by deliberately hurting the person or destroying the object of the anger. Children at a very early developmental level are not sufficiently aware of themselves and the world about them to get into purposeful fights. They respond to stress with a tantrum, and in distress and anger hit out. Similarly, children who are preoccupied with problems and unhappiness may have tantrums of distress, but are far less likely to fight. Other children never have tantrums, but are frequently involved in vicious kicking attacks and fights. They are beyond control, rather than in the out-of-control state of the temper tantrum. The motivation behind this behaviour is more complex; it is directed and purposeful and the aim is to destroy. Some of the children have temper tantrums *and* get into violent fights. These eruptions are commonly seen in children who cannot tolerate interference or having to share; they grab what they want or protect what they have, and a tantrum or fight ensues. They are also provoked by anything experienced as an attack or a threat. This could be an accidental touch or an ambiguous or innocent look, or the more straightforward name-calling.

Temper tantrums

Both mild and severe temper tantrums are characterized by rage and are usually triggered by frustration. Such children have an overwhelming need to take part, do what is required, or to achieve, but do not have the resources or confidence; their own wants are urgent and they cannot give way to anyone else.

A relatively minor difficulty sometimes triggers an outburst of shouting, screaming, crying and kicking. A feeling of anger that might get out of control is being conveyed. The adult can sometimes avert a tantrum or prevent it from escalating and getting out of control by holding the child's hands and, sensing the origin of the upset, describe the sequence of events leading up to it and how he feels, clearly and in detail. She continues to hold him as he struggles and resists and remains calm and waits. He is distracted relatively easily, and energy and angry feelings are diverted by asking him to stamp hard with his feet, and when he has released his feelings in this way, to stamp to the door and back. She manoeuvres him into the home area and settles him on the sofa, and he is left there to pummel the cushions. As soon as he is calm, the adult does what she can to make him feel wanted and valued, to re-establish the relationship. They talk about his feelings, and why he felt as he did and what he should do about it. Together they look in the mirror. He sees himself with the adult and takes in that he has an angry face but hers is relatively calm. Seeing how angry he looks helps him to objectify his feelings and learn about himself. He begins to calm down. She talks about how they look and the feelings they have. When he is himself again, he sees how different he looks and seems relieved. They spend a long time looking in the mirror, talking quietly; it is calm and peaceful. At no point is the child criticized or blamed.

Episodes of this kind soon disappear. They are more common in children from homes where opportunities are limited, but standards of behaviour are strict and uncompromising and expectations for achievement, high.

Sometimes the temper tantrums escalate so rapidly that all communication is lost and the children become completely out of control. The cause may be the frustration of trying to establish and assert their identity, excitement or a surge of anxiety or even panic that breaks through their fragile boundaries, or they may need an outlet for unbearable stress at home. Whatever the reason, these episodes are crisis points for the children concerned. If handled well, they are potentially the basis of a closer and more productive relationship because they demand close and total involvement from the adults. A temper tantrum of this nature is therefore accepted as a necessary contribution to children's immediate well-being and their future progress. It may nevertheless be stressful and alarming for them because the children are awash with uncontrolled feelings that have swept away their precariously held identity. They have no boundaries, no structure and the adults must provide them. It is therefore of vital importance that the adults do not lose control. If they become like the children, angry or frightened and filled with fear and panic, they will not be a secure identity against which children can define their own, and fear and panic will increase. They must be held, to contain and restrain them then, and to comfort them later when the storm is over. All the children need to see that the situation is under control, otherwise anxiety spreads and sometimes panic. But holding them is not always easy; many are big for their age, are strong and move with mercurial speed. Although these explosive outbursts are similar in quality to those normal at an earlier age, they are inevitably far more difficult to deal with. Usually, it is necessary for both adults to be involved and to act in concert.

Physical management of temper tantrums

The other children know what to do when a serious temper tantrum erupts because the adults have talked about this when they were quiet and attentive. If necessary, they are reminded:

- They move any chairs out of the way, move themselves away, taking their activity with them and continue with whatever they were doing.
- If possible, they face away from the scene of action and take no notice.
- The adult nearest to the child holds her/him.
- The other adult quickly removes any remaining obstructions or dangerous objects and as soon as possible gets close and tries to remove the child's shoes.

Events during a tantrum vary with children's physical strength and the extent to which they are out of control. If the tantrum is severe and the children are doing a lot of damage and are a danger to themselves and others, it is advisable to get them into a safer place – the home area if possible, or, alternatively, the other children can be taken outside, alerting another member of staff. A compromise is to take the child concerned or the other children out when the worst is over and one of the adults is available. At this stage, children are usually becoming more aware of themselves and separating them from the others spares them the shame of being seen in this state; it also makes it easier for them to rejoin them when they are calm again. If not kept apart, they are likely to feel self-conscious and become excited, fool about and have another tantrum later. By the time they are calm and with the others again, usually all of them behave as though nothing had happened.

Although often difficult to manage, a temper tantrum can nevertheless be helpful, for the others take in what is happening and realize that when they have a tantrum, they too look like that. In spite of instructions to the contrary, they stare and openly watch at first. As one child commented, when his own tantrums were a thing of the past, 'Miss, I used to be a bit like that', and the teacher remarked that he did not seem to like what he saw. The other children see how the adults behave, they realize that the adults are being controlled and considerate, not punitive or unkind, and this indirectly helps them when they are having a tantrum.

It is important that children in a tantrum are held and continue to be held. They need to be physically contained when emotionally in disorder but they might also run off. If they manage to free themselves, they are caught. Pursuing them is avoided if possible but there is risk of an accident and, apart from the danger, there is no possibility of bringing the episode to completion and restoring the relationship. Later on, at a time when everything is peaceful, it is usual for the teacher to talk to all the children as a group.

The trigger is usually some form of thwarting. It may be 'no' to something a child demands, constraint of some kind or another child being experienced as a threat. In other cases, the situation triggers pent-up anxiety and aggression and sometimes children seem subconsciously to be looking for a trigger. Experienced practitioners are alert and will:

• cope calmly and, if necessary, clamp the child's feet between their own for protection

- make physical contact, whether restraining or comforting. The child is 'lost'. All communication with others is also lost and physical contact is the first step in regaining attention and restoring communication and calm. If the adults are frightened or angry, the child experiences further loss of support
- continue to hold the child while attending to any other child who needs them; the others in an established group ignore minor tantrums. This maintains a matter-of-fact relationship and the struggling child may give partial attention to this and be momentarily drawn in
- try to anchor the child in reality by making factual comments or developing as a conversation any remark that is flung out or coolly asking diverting questions: 'What would you like to play with?' The aim is to maintain contact with reality and, if possible, break into the mounting loss of control
- comment factually on what is happening: 'You are feeling angry. I am holding your arms.' The child is probably screaming, kicking, biting. This is usual and is accepted as a stage in the development of self-control. The adult's objective continues to be to keep the situation as 'real' as possible, and so at this point the child might be asked to stand up. This deflects their attention and gives them something positive to do
- ask diverting questions and if the moment has been well chosen, the child replies. If this succeeds, they might try to limit the child's wild thrashing about by telling them to use their hands, not their feet. The aim is to constrain, limit and channel the aggression, which is now being expressed in random hitting, while at the same time legitimizing it. It might be suggested that the child hits the adult's hands, allowing them to show anger and aggression. This is the stage before turning the episode into a game. The adult has provided an alternative outlet and this has helped regain control
- limit the hurt and damage that could be caused by attempting verbally to restrict and direct the physical outburst. It is usual for a child in a tantrum to fall in with the adult's suggestion even while shouting out, 'No. No'. At this stage, the adult tries to make the situation increasingly 'real' by drawing attention to her/his own existence, 'to recover the person that is lost' (a head teacher).

Ending a tantrum

The ending of a tantrum is important. Children must be helped to accept and forget what has happened, and to know that the relationship and lost self-regard have been restored. The following anecdote describes the way in which a tantrum was brought to completion by the teacher and illustrates the relevance and importance of the many experiences that are built into a nurture group day.

The teacher in this group frequently engages the children in simple hand games which are introduced when the children are all together in the peace and quiet of the home area. The games are shared, intimate and enjoyable experiences in which skin contact and purposeful touch is made in fun and is associated with a close and supportive relationship with the adult. This is important because a child in a tantrum has to be held and although this physical contact is initially resisted, the earlier association with a secure and supportive relationship helps to make it tolerable and acceptable. These games are also important because a certain amount of aggression is allowed but is controlled by the rules of the game. In one of these games, the children in turn hit the teacher's hands, and she, theirs, in play. When one of the children in this group was having a tantrum towards the end, she offered her hands for him to hit. This distracted him, was a way of making skin and eye contact and provided an alternative in movement that legitimized and controlled his aggression. It gave him something positive to do and was a familiar activity associated with happy experiences and happy feelings in the home area. It was also part of a more elaborate game and the teacher could lead him further into this game which, because of its greater complexity, diverted his attention from his angry feelings. So when the teacher extended her hands, the child placed his on hers. He was familiar with this ritual and knew what to do. He clapped hard. This was allowed as it was felt to be a legitimate way for the child to assert himself and maintain his self-regard. He then tried to run off but the teacher pulled him back. He was about to clap again, hard, but the teacher controlled his aggression by saying, 'One second. I'm not ready'. The pause was momentary, but this time he gently put his hands on those of the teacher. She was in control and built in further control by saying, 'Slowly'. In this way, by introducing a familiar activity in which she, too, was involved, the teacher was able to impose manageable constraints and restore equilibrium. At the end of the tantrum episode, the teacher and child raised their hands together, fully stretched out, and slowly lowered them again, a movement that demanded considerable self-control. Their eyes met; they were held together in eye contact. They were fully in touch and there was a strong bond between them. They walked quietly out of the room, talking softly.

This way of ending the tantrum was idiosyncratic to the child and teacher concerned, but a ritualized ending is usual. Teachers stress the importance of this and the comfort it brings to the children who learn that it completes the episode, and so anticipate that the ending will come and that attachment to the teacher will be restored.

When the tantrum is over

Tantrums typically are followed by a quiet period. If a child has not been completely out of control, they may be receptive to comments at this stage, and so the adult explains what has happened, putting into words what it was that provoked the explosion and helping them to understand why. The adult comments on the feelings: 'You were angry.' Hand in hand, they look at the damage, not in a mood of criticism, but for the child to take it in. One child is likely to be subdued and afraid and another may be more self-aware and more aware of the adult, feel ashamed, embarrassed and guilty. Some children need reassurance, perhaps by telling them that they are often good but today they are angry. They cannot help feeling angry at times and the adult doesn't mind but next time they must go where they cannot hurt anyone and stamp and kick there. Together, they go to the corner and they both stamp in good humour. Finally: 'You were angry. Dry your tears. You feel better now.' The aim when talking about the tantrum afterwards is to convey that the adults care about them even though they have bad feelings and tantrums. At the same time, they make them aware of the consequences of their behaviour, and the reality of the damage done. They are not criticized, but there is the implicit assumption that they want to grow out of the tantrums, and will. The adults might go on to develop the idea of give and take, or the need to share and not get angry and grab. They have to listen to what the other person says and sort it out.

Very severe tantrums

Tantrums in which the child is completely out of control are more difficult to manage. Usually, the same kind of simple frustrating incident triggers the outburst. In some cases, this seems to provide a release for pent-up frustration and anger that has its origin beyond the immediate situation. The temper tantrum that ensues can be severe and might go on, with only short-lived lulls, for an hour or more. The management problems are considerable.

In a tantrum, Joseph is extremely difficult to hold, seems completely out of touch with his surroundings and with himself, and sometimes goes berserk and destroys everything in his path. His kicks and bites have superhuman force and he screams, swears, scratches, shouts abuse and hurls anything at hand, frequently yelling, 'You all hate me'. If the tantrum is a very bad and aggressive one, the assistant attempts to take him outside. He is held but struggles, thrashes around and may knock some furniture over. 'Let me go.' 'When you've quietened down.' 'Let me go.' 'If you stop struggling, I will let you go.' He shouts 'Yes. Yes', but not necessarily indicating that he will stop struggling; he is trusted, but the adult lets go of one arm only, talking to him all the time, saying: 'I am letting you go, but you must keep still.' If he renews his struggles when one arm is released, the arm is caught and held once again. This might be repeated two or three times. 'When you've quietened down, we'll talk about it. We'll talk about it and sort it out.'

Discussion is not helpful at this stage because he is not capable of giving attention. It is often three-quarters of an hour before he quietens down but he eventually gives up, worn out and panting, exhausted, limp and damp with sweat. He cries. At this point, he will go into the corner or sit in an armchair, screwed up, legs drawn up to his chin, sucking his thumb.

After a tantrum, the children want to be on their own for five or ten minutes. They are withdrawn and anti-everything. A frequent comment is 'I don't care' but they seem sad and even while saying this might cry. 'Would you like … ?' 'No.' 'Would you … ?' 'No.' Children in this mood are best left, but very soon are approachable, cuddle up and can be talked to. The adult mops their brow as a reminder of the consequences of a tantrum and part of the process of reconciliation. Sometimes both have a wash. After a tantrum, they might go for a walk around the school, looking at the pictures on the walls, and the adult keeps a conversation going by talking about them; or the child might cuddle up in sadness and exhaustion and go to sleep. The adults like to keep the children with them until they are quiet, gentle and responsive. They judge how best to clear up any wreckage. If appropriate, they will clear up together but the action of clearing up is not used as a punishment for the tantrum even though it is a consequence. The adults or the other children clear up, rather than risk further humiliation or negativism in the child. Often, the most reassuring and comforting way, particularly if the child feels guilty, is for the adult and child to clear up together when the upset is over. The child feels calm, attached and dependent, and may feel better doing it alone, by way of restitution.

After a bad outburst, particularly if more than one child is involved, they may not be in a state to talk about what happened. The scene in the classroom may appear idyllic, with children who shortly before were totally out of control, sitting at the teacher's feet, drained of life and very dependent and loving. Later, there is talk about what happened, what started it off, the feelings they had, and what they can do about it. For example, next time they suddenly feel full of these feelings, they must pick up the cushion and thump that, or bang their fists on the floor, or clench them and say how angry they feel. If they want to, they can go and tell the teacher or assistant how angry they feel, and what it was that made them angry. Bad language is accepted as the next stage in learning self-control, but some teachers suggest something inconsequential and humorous for them to say.

Together they work out what happened

The precipitating cause of these outbursts is in many cases very simple, and the teacher works on it later. With older children, whether involved in fights or tantrums, more discussion is possible and it is usual for this to involve the whole group. The teacher helps the children with the words they need and every child has a chance to say what happened. Gradually, they become aware of their behaviour and try to control themselves. They seem to know that the teacher is providing a learning experience. After criticism, where before they would have a tantrum, they have said, 'I'm not having a tantrum'. This change happens because the adults provide support and reassurances, put everything into words, and are consistent in their response. The children take in that the adults do not get angry and are not punitive. They accept their requirements and begin to learn to regulate their own behaviour. When this stage is reached, they seem more aware of themselves: one child, when seeing another in a tantrum, said: 'Miss, it's a nice feeling, being good.' But anger in the adult can be helpful when the child is giving vicious vent to angry feelings, and knows it, and is capable of doing better.

Fights

The children who get into fights are more easily provoked and for less rational reasons than is usual for their age. Any controls they have internalized are not sufficient to contain their distress and fury and a fight erupts.

Fights frequently have their origin in distress of some kind but not always. Some of the children, particularly if older, are well organized at a level of basic survival. They are alert to defend themselves from anything they sense as potential attack, forestall this by attacking first and retaliation follows. With lightning speed, the whole group can be involved, bodies and chairs hurtle across the room and any equipment close at hand is seized and used as a weapon.

Fights are difficult to deal with because the children quickly get out of control, have more than usual strength and 'There is hate in their eyes and they kick to kill' (a KS2 teacher). They can do a great deal of damage to each other and to their surroundings. The wear and tear on the adults is considerable, particularly in older groups where aggressive behaviour is more likely to erupt and the children are bigger and stronger.

Fortunately, children who have reached the level of purposeful fights have some concept of themselves in relation to others, and to some extent can follow an explanation and grasp a simple sequence of events. So, from the beginning, when the children are in the home area or at the table having their drink and biscuits, there is firm talk about fights, and the things that upset them. The adults make clear that fights are not acceptable and have to stop. They:

- put feelings into words by drawing attention to unacknowledged feelings, identifying them so children become more aware of their feelings and are better able to control them
- suggest alternatives to hitting out or fighting, in the hope that a constructive response will eventually be built in
- ritualize fighting by having formal play fights with special 'gear' (perhaps team bands), rituals and rules. If there is a flare-up in the group, and indications that a fight might break out, the children are encouraged to turn the incident into a game
- control aggression by introducing rules which formalize it. The children are required to stop at the end of each round and start again only when a signal is given, or they are expected to keep inside a chalk square. The children pay attention to the imposed conditions and accept them
- provide rules and ritual interest for the children who are watching; they concentrate on the rules rather than the fight, and exercise control by seeing that the rules are kept and insist that they are kept
- turn a primitive fight into a contest with rules putting a controlling brake on the children, slowing them down and helping to contain their aggression which now has a legitimate outlet and is not immediately discharged in unacceptable action
- provide limits; accepting and remembering the limits keeps feelings under control. When other children are fighting, they will be the ones to impose and maintain the limits, and this reinforces their own limits because of the satisfaction of providing limits for others.

Experience of the double process of imposing and accepting

limits helps them to internalize controls and to internalize a notion of authority that is more subtle than one of unilateral power. This way of managing fights demonstrates a fundamental process in the functioning of nurture groups: the adults accept the child's level of development but build in tolerable constraints.

Preventing fights wherever possible

The adults are constantly alert to any incident that could escalate and, whenever possible, they prevent fights by their rapid intervention. But fights do break out and, as with tantrums, the other children ignore them, move away and carry on with their activities. Some of these children are liable to get into fights themselves at other times, but they are greatly aff-ronted when their activities are disturbed by fights and they complain. This is a useful learning experience, for they see what a fight is like, see the aftermath and get some understanding of the implications for others and the reason for the 'no fighting' rule. What happens next depends on the potential violence of the fight. If the adults know from their experience of the children concerned that they are likely to do little more than punch each other and cry and will do little damage, they are left. They give their attention and interest to the children who are playing and working. Minor injuries, complaints and appeals to the adults for retribution are ignored or rejected. If it is necessary to tend an injury, no tenderness or sympathy is expressed, and any feeling shown is of displeasure. An exception is made where the fight is clearly unfair, either because one child is being attacked without cause, or he is at a severe disadvantage because of size and strength. If the fight continues at an infantile, passionate level but is not completely out of hand, the teacher might try to influence the situation indirectly by collecting the other children together for a story or other pleasurable activity. The aim is to create a close-knit family situation in which security and satisfaction are at a high level, with the hope that this peacefulness and the strength of the attachment of these children to the adult will influence the behaviour of those who are fighting. Later, the fighters get the interest and attention when they are doing something constructive.

Management of fights

If the fight seems to be potentially dangerous, the adults, sometimes with the help of the other children, move anything dangerous that could be used as a weapon out of the way. Most fights, particularly among older children, become violent. There is risk of injury, and if the adults know that the children concerned will 'fight to the death' (a teacher), it will be necessary to try to separate them and hold them, usually by each one standing behind a child, arms clasped round their elbows, pinning their arms back. As with temper tantrums, the adults avoid the full force of a kick. The children, however, remain face to face and get relief for their feelings by snarling and spitting at each other. Each adult speaks quietly to the child, giving simple, positive, calming instructions. It is important that adults learn the knack of physically disengaging and holding the children, if possible removing their shoes while remaining emotionally uninvolved and calm. They try to look calm, for if they betray anxiety, distress or anger, the situation is likely to worsen. Once the fighters have been separated, one may feel satisfied and ready to give up, but the other might still be angry and need undivided attention for about 15 minutes afterwards. The adults are alert and at an appropriate moment might offer to read the child a story and the mood slowly dissipates. The children concerned usually avoid each other for a time but are soon together again, the upset forgotten. After a bad fight, children who are still enraged are given a space to 'cool off'. This is done in a neutral, matter-of-fact way. They still have contact with the group but are physically distanced from it.

Talking through the incident

Afterwards, the adults ask: 'Why did it happen?' They bring the children involved into the discussion and help them to see how it happened and what went wrong.

They look at the problem from everyone's perspective and put it into words for them. Everyone has a time to talk. This has to be strictly controlled because they are all likely to talk at once. It is always everyone else's fault and they sit and fume as they hear the lies all the others tell. They protest and are outraged, and when their turn comes, the others protest and are outraged. They are not allowed to interrupt. Each child is heard out and his version is pieced together, no matter how long it takes. The teacher marshals the evidence and pulls it together, and remains with the children until it is sorted out and feelings have simmered down. The issue is usually very simple. One child might have been jumped on in friendly exuberance but thought he was being attacked. To emphasize the serious nature of the occasion, the children sit on chairs and sometimes to make the occasion more formal they are taken into the library. The teacher gets out paper and pencil, writes down everything they say and reads it back to them in order to gain their full attention and make the situation more important and more real.

With patience and time, they can be helped to understand what happened and seem to accept comments such as, 'We won't let that happen again, will we?' They might be fighting again a few days later but the problem does not worsen. Later on, and this might be as long as two terms for some of the more difficult older children, they are left with the problem after a disturbance, and with minimal direction are able to sort it out for themselves. When the adults feel they have begun to accept their reasoning and they complain again, they tell them they are tired of sorting out squabbles and that they have to work it out for themselves. Later, as the disputes became more reasonable and involve more complex and subtle issues, they are encouraged to turn to the adults for help.

Fighting does not stop immediately, and might even get worse for a while; some groups reach a peak of bad behaviour, fights and tantrums before suddenly calming down and consolidating. Even when a group appears to have calmed down, there may be occasional less serious outbreaks of fighting.

The task for the adults in sorting out the disputes that lead to fighting is made easier because the children have a keen sense of fairness. When they understand the point the adults are making and begin to see that they are impartial and everyone is treated the same way, they accept the sanctions. Nevertheless, for a long time, they conform only because of the sanctions and are slow to acknowledge and accept responsibility for their actions.

Providing other outlets

Fighting has to be controlled because it goes well beyond normal acceptable limits but physical outlets too must be provided, because opportunities for active play are often very limited. Children may come into school in a highly charged state, very resentful and angry, and need some means of expressing their feelings. Indoors, a trampoline used under controlled conditions, and a punch bag, are helpful for older children. Ideally, the nurture group room should open onto a playground, preferably an enclosed area, where the children can run when they are irritable and restless.

Summary ☐

- Nurture group practitioners are prepared for the possibility of temper tantrums and fights but take steps to avoid them wherever possible.
- They understand the causes and what might trigger an outburst.
- Feelings are put into words and alternative outlets are provided.
- Practitioners have confidence in the school policy and procedures for managing incidents and the other children are taught how to respond.
- Talking through incidents afterwards enables children to move on; there is no criticism or blame, endings are ritualized and reconciliation is appropriate for the individual.

Further reading

DCSF (2007) *The Use of Force to Control or Restrain Pupils.* London: The Stationery Office. Check your school policy and procedures comply with the up-to-date guidance from the relevant government department.

Gerhardt, S. (2004) *Why Love Matters: How Affection Shapes a Baby's Brain.* Hove and New York: Brunner-Routledge. Part 2 of this book provides insight into the roots of behaviour disorders.

Ofsted (2005) *Managing Challenging Behaviour.* London: HMI. Nurture group practice is much more detailed but this might be helpful for a wider audience as are the SEAL resources at www. nationalstrategies.standards.dcsf.gov.uk

6

Earliest Learning Experiences

This chapter describes how the developing child is shaped by experiences from birth and even before:

- At the earliest stage, experiences come through close physical and emotional attachment to the parent, the satisfactions of warmth and food, and with this, a sense of well-being.
- As children begin to explore within the security of a close, holding and sustaining relationship with a supportive, caring, responsive adult, their experiences widen and become more complex and organized.
- The early nurturing relationship the adults provide, and the experiences they make available and support, have essential and fundamental content for the development of a sense of self, interpersonal relationships and cognitive competence.
- Nurture group practitioners relate to the children at the developmentally appropriate stage whatever their age; they replicate these missed early learning experiences in the nurture curriculum (see Chapter 1 – Earliest learning: a summary chart, p. 7).

Earliest needs and interests: the nurture curriculum

The earliest learning need is for attachment but it is unusual for children coming into the nurture group to make a normal attachment relationship with the adults.

Some children attach themselves to any adult indiscriminately in seeking affection and attention, or make a strong attachment with one adult
and seek reassurance all the time. Most, however, mistrust adults, have
profound difficulty in relating to them and no natural desire to please
them. Frequently, they are indifferent to their presence or may totally
ignore them. They rarely make normal eye contact, but glance around
indiscriminately, or defensively look away from the teacher or fixedly
through her. Many of them dislike physical contact and avoid it, or they
actively resist touch and shrug off the adult's arm. Others accept physical contact, but never show a need for it. Others again tentatively put
an arm round the adult and touch their hand and face, but are self-
conscious and uncomfortable, particularly the older children, if others
see them doing this, and they withdraw quickly if the adult gives any
sign of having noticed.

For a small number of children, attempts to encourage eye contact
and touch are an intolerable intrusion.

Establishing eye contact and touch

This is one of the practitioners' first aims; it is built in purposefully
but tentatively.

Few of the children at first make normal eye contact but this
is usually established fairly quickly, largely because the adults
address and look at each child directly and individually, and
meticulously respond to any eye contact made by them (see
Chapter 3).

Touch, too, is avoided at first, but is acceptable to most of the
children if initiated tentatively in play such as a foot-touching
game with shoes on before skin contact is made. For some
children, reasons may have to be contrived at other times for
spontaneous physical contact (see Chapter 3).

The need for physical contact with the adults is a general one
in primary age groups. The nature of the need and the level of
the contact varies: for some children, it seems primarily a need
for reassurance and affection, and the pleasure of showing
affection, while others seem to need to attach themselves
passively, to saturate themselves in comfort, peace and well-
being.

Some children physically cling to the adult. Sometimes, when the teacher reads to a child on her lap, the others draw close and put their hands round her neck and snuggle up or lean towards her. There might be three or four draped over her, while others sit on the floor by her feet and touch her shoes. Some of the children at times seem totally absorbed in the adult's appearance and will comment on the colour of her eyes, notice her earrings, what she is wearing and even the smell of her perfume. The child will often become totally absorbed and fascinated by the appearances and nuances of the adult in the group. He/she is developing the ability to evaluate and understand others using all their senses, an ability which usually develops at a much younger age (Gerhardt, 2004).

Recapturing the baby state

Other children, perhaps only fleetingly, seem to need to attach themselves as a baby would, and are like babies or toddlers in the way they behave and communicate. These features are particularly marked in some of the children described as aggressive and disruptive; whether KS1 or 2, descriptions of these children are remarkably similar.

Often, the overriding need for physical contact in children can be very strong and adults working in nurture groups need to be aware of this. Practitioners have commented that this is not exploration: 'They seem to be taking in the warmth, taking in what a living person is, and with contact discovering the complexities of another human being'. They describe children clinging to them as young babies do and slipping into baby babbling sounds. Many of them suck their fingers or thumbs, or put everything into their mouths. They may try to put on younger clothes and ask to be fed. The other children seem unconcerned by this behaviour; they accept it and treat them as younger in their role play.

A developmental progression from the baby stage is seen to a striking extent in children who seem out of contact when admitted to the group and in those who are more involved but interfere with the others and readily erupt into temper tantrums. The children 'egress' through these stages very quickly; the 'baby' stage is truly a baby stage. The children are not *being* babyish, nor are they role-playing babies. They *are* babies, in the behavioural characteristics they show. This is seen most clearly in children who, from the evidence available, have been markedly restricted at home when they were beginning to be physically mobile.

More usually, baby behaviour and communication take longer to appear and last intermittently for a longer time. These children are developmentally more advanced, and are more accurately described as regressing to an earlier stage rather than egressing to a later one.

Immature mannerisms are sometimes seen in KS2 and 3 children. They shout in the adult's face, interrupt, prod and tug at their sleeves but when a hand is held out to them without speaking, they will take hold and wait.

Baby and toddler behaviour is usually short-lived

Baby and toddler features are usually relatively short-lived, and a child might be at this level for 20 minutes or so in the group, and be throwing stones and swearing in the playground later. This stage is normally fairly quickly outgrown, and a child showing this behaviour to a marked extent goes from baby attachment to toddler movements, in less than a month. Such children are usually ready to go into a mainstream class within a year, by which time they will have learned to tolerate interference and upsets, often after a period of tantrums. The following description, of a child who went rapidly through these early stages, was provided by his teacher.

> From the first days in the nurture group, Ricky behaved like a baby of nine months. He sat like a baby, his face expressive and animated, with the toys around him, and enjoyed throwing them onto the floor for the teacher or assistant to pick up. He babbled and gurgled, crawled about making baby noises, used single exclamations by way of comment, and enjoyed simple games like peek-a-boo. He liked to be

near the adults, pulled at them to attract their attention and enjoyed physical contact. He didn't involve himself with the other children but watched them, fascinated. Otherwise, he played by himself, repetitively and unimaginatively, with simple toys and objects, sometimes throwing or dropping them, talking to himself a great deal. The baby phase lasted only one or two weeks. After that, he was more active, and playing and conversing in the role-play area. He painted, and played with the cars and construction activities, sand, water and dough, interacting to some extent with the other children, and was friendly and likeable. He was affectionate with the adults and tried hard to please, but always seemed on the verge of a tantrum or explosion.

Practitioners have remarked that a 'fantastic' relationship develops with children who go through these early stages: 'We seem to sense each other's feelings.'

Making relationships: different levels

Most of the children form a close relationship with both adults but the physical attachments they make appear to express different levels of need. In KS1 and some KS2 groups, virtually all the children make a close baby/ toddler level of attachment; in others, a close warm relationship, as with a child in the nursery, is more usual.

Relationships: learning to share the teacher

This close contact means a great deal to the children. If a child becomes insistent in their demands, as when a situation outside of school has become intolerable, some of the others get jealous. The adult is alert to these feelings and helps them to make sense of them. This closeness shows the child that their worries are recognized and they will be helped to understand them. In making explicit the need to share, the children become more aware of their feelings and the needs of others, and this helps them to accept that others need affection and attention, too.

A sensory environment and learning

Sensory experiences, such as touching, feeling, hearing and smelling, are another important feature of early development and learning. Discovering and exploring textures, colour, sound and movement are all part of everyday experience that babies and toddlers use to begin to understand the world around them.

Nurture group children have usually missed these vital sensory experiences and they need opportunities to revisit them with an adult. Some nurture groups are being developed with a sophisticated professionally designed and built sensory room, but a typical nurture environment also provides a wealth of simple sensory opportunities, for example:

- the feel of different materials against the skin, crumpled against the face, smelt, stroked and worn
- the feel and texture of clay, play dough, shaving foam, etc. – not for model making but for squishing, rolling and shaping
- the exploration of a treasure or discovery basket, slowly, with items being added and removed at different times over a period of weeks
- the sound and use of simple percussion instruments in games and songs
- the discovery of 'what's in the bag?' – feely items, noisy items, plastic animals, etc.
- the discovery of 'what is it?' using a blindfold – always adult-led and only when a child is ready
- sand and water play – inside and out – with hands to begin with and moving on to toys and equipment.

In a mainstream classroom sensory play at this level would be seen as an indiscriminate use of resources and therefore destructive but nurture group children need these opportunities for exploratory play which is the foundation for their future learning and development.

Safeguarding and promoting the welfare of children

All children are fascinated by each other's bodies, however a few children demonstrate sexual interest of a different order. There is a marked component of more overt and intense sexualized involvement, occasionally shown in histrionic posturing or overt sexual display and invitation, and sometimes sexualized excitement is an element in their aggressive physical attacks on each other. In the safe and secure environment of the nurture group, some children will disclose and even exhibit sexual behaviour. The school's policies and procedures for safeguarding children are a protection for staff as well as children; nurture practitioners should know them and the named members of the senior management team with whom to discuss their concerns.

Physical self-care

Some of the children will not have acquired some of the basic life skills, e.g. dressing/undressing. As with every new learning experience, the adults break the task down into stages; they talk through the specific detail or provide visual prompts, with encouraging comments at every step taken. Some children need help in managing themselves at the toilet. Cutlery may present difficulties; they need to be shown how to manage the food, whether eating a piece of toast or getting a spoonful of cereal into their mouths.

Transitional objects

Most young children like to carry around or sleep with a comfort object but by the time they start school, most are happy to leave them at home. In the nurture group, the children express their close relationship to the adults by making use of some of their personal items, which seem to be a source of security, comfort and control. Such things serve as the 'transitional objects' described by Winnicott (1971) and are particularly important to nurture children when they are beginning to manage on their own without the immediate support of the adults. They take personal things from the adults to wear, often jewellery and detachable garments such as scarves, and use them as though they feel them to be part of the adults. They have special meaning because they are invested with the idea and feeling of the adults.

Victor was fascinated by the teacher's large clip-on earrings and touched them often. He asked to wear them and went into assembly with them on. All the children had been interested in the teacher's earrings, and had lovingly commented that they were nice. One by one, they wore the earrings, taking turns and sharing them all day long. This was the first instance of sharing in this group. In a very real sense, they were sharing the teacher because the earrings represented her presence and her support.

These naturally arising links with the adult are of great value, for they not only provide satisfaction, well-being and security but also carry their expectations and standards. They are objects of control as well as comfort and they are enabling objects, as they help the children to function on their own at a higher and more organized level than might otherwise be possible. Because of their importance, they are often deliberately introduced by the teacher, and are accompanied by a verbal message. These messages are, by association with the object, a more sophisticated form of transitional object, and their function is a more explicit monitoring of the child's behaviour. At the simplest level, the teacher might make a comment about being tidy when tying on the child's painting apron. Comment and apron would, in effect, be tied on together.

Transitional objects help change

As teachers become accustomed to providing support through transitional objects, they begin to plan their use to manage new situations and the transitions which are part of everyday life at home and at school, from going home at the end of a day to moving house.

The predictability of routines in the nurture group helps children's development (see Chapter 3); knowing what to expect gives a sense of security, a feeling of safety, and it helps children manage stress and cope with change. Many children cope with some major changes in their lives but nurture group children often experience a life so out of their control and unsupported that any change, however small, is a cause of stress. Transitional objects can be used by the adults to provide support for children during major transitions such as family breakdowns, bereavements and moving house.

Transitions or changes in the school day, too, require gentle management and doing things in small steps can be a preparation for bigger changes elsewhere. Having cues to prepare them for a change is useful. For instance, a small change during a session might be identified by:

- a song, playing music, or ringing a chime to move from one activity to the other
- a 'warning' at the ten-minute mark, and the three-minute mark.

The story of Ali, a Y3 child, illustrates the use of a transitional object to help him be calm and become part of school life beyond the nurture group.

Ali was a child without boundaries; he was suspicious of everyone and everything. He was a 'loner' and conformity of any description was out of the question.

Over a term, Ali started to develop trust and acceptance within the nurture group but elsewhere in the school he posed an enormous problem to staff and children alike, especially in assembly where he had to sit with his year group. Unless he had one-to-one supervision, he would shout, poke children around him, roll around and pull faces. He knew this would ensure that he would be removed and return to the nurture group with the assistant where he felt secure and at ease. It was decided to introduce a transitional object to help him deal with the change that was involved in leaving the nurture group room and going to the hall for 20 minutes.

The teacher started by talking through her expectations with all the children every day, five minutes before leaving the nurture room. She reminded them of what would happen, what was involved and that they would have breakfast when they returned. Breakfast was rescheduled to allow this to happen on assembly days. Ali was given the nurture group door key to look after, safely ready for use after assembly. Trust was involved in this. It was placed on a ribbon around his wrist and he was reminded to keep it safe. He would look at the key to remind him that he would be returning to the nurture room and also how he should behave in assembly. After some weeks, Ali would take the key and put it in his pocket, producing it at the end of assembly for the teacher to use. Eventually, the key became irrelevant as he began to accept assembly as part of his school day and he attended appropriately.

A remarkable example of the significance to the child of a transitional object provided to help him manage on his own was described by the teacher of a KS1 group.

> Bkongo, a six-year-old boy, was again one of the most aggressive children in the group. He was being 'weaned' into his mainstream class and from time to time was there for half a day. On the occasion concerned, his teacher, as was customary, gave him one of her bracelets to provide support. Instead of going off to his class, he lingered, and said: 'Please can I have two bracelets today. There are two difficult things to do.' There were two difficult things to do because it was a rainy day, and he was not only going into his mainstream class but would be there during a wet playtime. This anecdote vividly illustrates the remarkable insight Bkongo had into his awareness of stress and his need for extra help, and the significance to him of the transitional object provided by the teacher.

Personal possessions as a means of communication

Small items or inconsequential things such as a feather found during the course of the day become important personal possessions. They are intimately part of the child and are sometimes used as a communication between children and adults, and, in so far as they represent the child, are a giving and a taking of their feelings and needs. It is common when the children first join the group for them to entrust nothing to the teacher, but soon they are secure enough to give her their precious things for safe-keeping. This is sometimes the first indication of a relationship.

> The importance of this safe-keeping was seen in a KS2 group where it was customary for the children to leave their small belongings such as cards, sweets and pieces of string in the pocket of the teacher's yellow canvas bag, to be collected at the end of the day. Whenever the children were restless and excited, the teacher put these in a row on the low table in front of her while she read them a story, and this always settled them down. The safe-keeping of their little treasures was in a very real way a safe-keeping of themselves, and when put on the table were a visible demonstration of trust and attachment.

Moods and feelings are sometimes expressed through objects that have 'attachment' significance for the child.

> A six-year-old brought into school a trinket ring belonging to the aunt who was looking after him and said to his teacher: 'You wear it today. I brought it for you.' Later, he was cross and asked for it back. Five minutes later, he said: 'You have it back. I will be good.'

The ring expresses his attachment to his aunt and teacher, and his awareness of its value in helping him to control his feelings.

A comforting place

Sometimes the children 'need to get away from it all, and curling up on the sofa may be the only place in their lives where it is possible' (a teacher). It is comforting to lie on the sofa covered by a blanket as if in bed. Sometimes children cry there after an upsetting incident. They cuddle up with a soft toy and like to be tucked in with a blanket and have the adult sit with them and read a story.

Play

Many of the children have an initial lack of interest in dolls. A few show some interest when the adult nurses the doll, but on the whole they have no interest in nursing it themselves. Instead, they wield the dolls as weapons, kick them about or ignore them. They seem to move on to doll play and caring for the dolls only after their own need for affection has been met. Big soft toys seem far more important to them.

Large soft toys: making physical contact and expressing feelings

Children of all ages, including KS3, who find physical contact difficult at first may find a large soft toy unthreatening. Ideally, this is soft, firm and friendly looking. Rag dolls, animals and teddy bears are comfortable and comforting, but are also the object and vehicle of fierce, raw feelings of love and hate. They are hugged, cuddled and put to bed, and with a rapid switch of mood have been stamped on, beaten and punched, put in prison, or tied in a bag and thrown away, or soon forgotten. Often they are fought over.

The toy becomes personalized

The children's relationship with a soft toy becomes more personal in time. It is a member of the group, is hugged and fought, sometimes in front of the mirror. Often, they are given personal names; they sit with the children at storytime, are put to bed, eat with them and are fed, sometimes before they take food for themselves. They seem particularly important in groups of older children when they are doing curriculum work and sometimes sit at the table or are given a book to read. In some cases, the toy seems to represent the child; they express through it an awareness of their own behaviour, for example by smacking it for something they have done wrong.

The toy is a support for 'good' behaviour and an outlet for aggression

The adults use soft toys to support children in a difficult situation. The toy may be used to express approval or disapproval: he sits at the breakfast table with the children but leaves them if they are rowdy and comes back only when they are quiet again.

A large soft toy is sometimes used by the adults to rid children of aggressive feelings. They personalize the toy and encourage them to use it as a punch bag, and a child might of their own accord attack it.

Stimulating speech, language and communication through a soft toy

Approximately 7 per cent of five-year-olds entering school in 2007 (nearly 40,000 children) and 50 per cent of children and young people in some socio-economically disadvantaged areas had significant speech, language and communication difficulties (DCSF, 2008b: 14). Some children admitted to nurture groups have never been heard to speak. There are many examples of practitioners stimulating them to speak by animating a soft toy animal.

> Sid didn't speak and barely participated in group activities. His teacher used a soft toy rabbit to 'steal' his bricks, talking through the rabbit as she did so: 'Give them to me. I want them.' He giggled and defended himself verbally. The teacher egged him on, using the rabbit's voice. She suggested different ways of telling the rabbit off, and he took these up spontaneously. Since then, he has been giving the adults scraps of news. The teacher used more baby/toddler level games and interactions and he continued to make progress. He was now speaking more in his base class, even putting up his hand to answer questions, and his mother reported progress at home.

Development of caring through play

Interest in dolls comes later. The children treat them as babies, though usually are rough with them at first, bash them when they cry, and turn them face down or throw them away. When they are making food, 'the baby' is sometimes fed, and the baby is the doll, or a passive child in the group. Gradually, this play develops as each child is helped along by the needs of the others, by the new ideas and associations and feelings evoked by the adults in the comments they make and by the children's deepening security as they move on from needing care to giving care. This kind of transition was seen vividly in a KS2 group, where one boy who had repeatedly climbed into the pram was, within two terms, pushing the nurture group pet around in the pram with supervision.

> A realistic doll 'baby', can be invaluable in the development of caring. In a KS1 group, all the children treated one as a real baby. One of the girls was jealous, and sat on the teacher's knee, cuddling it and sucking her fingers, but even she loved the 'baby' and cared for it. The children tiptoed about not wanting to wake the baby up and they tenderly cleaned its eyes, ears and nose with wisps of cotton wool. They were very gentle with it, there was a remarkably close family feeling and the boys for the first time were involved with a doll. Interestingly, all these children had been through a baby stage.

Caring for plants and animals is important in KS2 and 3 groups but usually comes later for younger children.

Developing play: adult support

The children initially need help in using toys and equipment and in developing their play; when left on their own, their activity usually remains limited and repetitive. They exhaust the possibilities of each situation very quickly, need to be constantly supplied with something to do and provided with ideas. The adults model for them how they think, feel and behave and they promote concept development and reasoning skills by:

- involving themselves in the children's play whenever this is possible and appropriate, helping and demonstrating
- introducing ideas, giving guidance and direction, identifying with the activity as a parent would, sharing and enjoying the experience with them
- giving a running commentary
- asking questions and answering them
- expressing their thoughts aloud as they think through a problem
- verbalizing their feelings when something goes wrong: 'but never mind, we'll try again.'

Solitary play

At first, play is usually solitary and content-poor. The children have little awareness of others; they do not spontaneously adjust their position in relation to another child playing nearby and are liable to erupt if accidentally touched. They are given their own protected play space, usually on the carpet, and here many of them engage in solitary repetitive play day after day, e.g. shape sorting, construction and jigsaws, but always on their own. In the playground, too, they often play alone. The children need time and space for these solitary activities. The adults do not intrude, but maintain a watching brief, ready when appropriate to offer suggestions or another toy.

Playing alongside

Play gradually develops and becomes more enriched and elaborate over time as the children get used to playing alongside each other. They pursue their own theme, but very gradually become involved in each other's play. When left to play at their own level alongside children playing at a similar level, with familiar material which gives them the satisfaction of success, they notice and comment, and begin to offer suggestions, and to copy. Each gains from the other.

Cooperative to collaborative play

Cooperative play develops as one child becomes interested in the others' play, watches for a moment, appreciates what is happening and joins in. The play gradually becomes more complex and increasingly elaborate as the children incorporate each other's ideas, and many of them begin to take on roles and act out their feelings. The transition comes about with relatively little guidance from the adults, though they make frequent observations. With support, the children's play moves from solitary to alongside, to cooperative then finally collaborative as they begin to incorporate one another's ideas to produce something entirely new.

When the children are constructively and imaginatively involved with each other, a minimal contribution from the adult can enable them to support and further each other's play. Play can also be facilitated by others who are more advanced, and sometimes it is helpful to plan and include children from mainstream classes who would benefit.

Role play

For many children, role play at first focuses on food. They spend a lot of time making and serving food and this theme is particularly persistent with the more dependent children. Although two or three of them might be busy with this activity, they are frequently not involved with each other, except in so far as they are giving or receiving food. Children who play at a more complex and imaginative level might be involved to some extent with each other in their play, but rarely sustain this because they quarrel and turn on each other. Very quickly, however, they begin to play quietly and constructively together. Often, the themes developed are domestic ones or may be hospitals, schools and the hairdressers; they drive make-believe buses, police cars and fire engines, and pretend to be any current figures of interest to them. Although play is often at early years or KS1 level, the most important aspect may be its nurture content. Hairdressing and hospitals, for example, involve physical contact, caring and being cared for, and provide sensory experience, language and communication dev-elopment, extend self-image, and increase self-regard and awareness of others, as well as requiring sustained attention and fine motor control. They also lend themselves to other curriculum-related areas.

Hiding and finding play

A sturdy cardboard box is needed for the children to curl up inside in total containment and seclusion or to use for jack-in-the-box play. Bigger cardboard boxes are useful to get in and out of and to hide in. Sometimes the children curl up as though in a cot or use them as boats or cars. Most children like to build tiny enclosed spaces, with walls, covered with blankets to make camps or caves; they hide away under the blanket all alone or crawl under tables and into hidey-holes. Often, they draw the adults directly into their play, for example by hiding away and asking to be 'found'. The adults provide ideas and create images, and in their comments on feelings and relationships, they increase the children's aware-ness of themselves and each other.

Creative play

Creative play develops in the nurture group because of the avail-ability of toys and resources at the appropriate developmental level and which the children can use according to their need. The support and involvement of the adult are crucial to developing the creativity and imagination of young children, which are impor-tant for all their other learning (Duffy, 1998). As time goes on, the children assimilate ideas from stories, outings and conversation, and their play develops as they become aware of the possibilities of the resources. They begin to interact constructively and imaginatively with each other, and at this stage it is more usual to leave them to play on their own. For older children, art, drama and music may be planned to have similar nurture content.

Children of all ages may occasionally revert to an earlier level. In one KS2 group, simple basic water play was a recurring need, and the same nine- and ten-year-olds, after a period of more advanced play, made pull-along toys by tying string to model cars and charged about the room with them. Teachers stress that it is not enough to give the children time to develop their play and learn to play together successfully – 'they need time to experience the joy of successful play' (a teacher).

Play as an outlet for stress

Play also provides some of the children with a way of working through their turbulent feelings. The feelings expressed are not always negative. Sometimes a child seems to be caring for himself, or is consolidating his social behaviour through the toy. A stressful event in the child's life, or an amorphous fear of frightening things, is sometimes spontaneously acted out.

Occasionally, a child suddenly initiates a play theme of a more vividly personal nature and, with no involvement on the part of the adults, plays through a situation of severe stress or the feelings associated with it with dramatic improvement in attitude and well-being. Presumably this happens because in the more controlled but relaxed atmosphere of the nurture group, his play is protected from the intrusion of others, and he is secure enough to demonstrate his difficulties and fears in his play.

Activities that become a stereotyped routine

Some activities become a repetitive, stereotyped routine. Construction is an example. Some children enjoy and settle into it; it gives security and is restricted but can be extended with the adult's help. An agreement can be made where they make their model because this is something *they* want to do, but they are then encouraged to attempt something more creative because this is what the adults want them to do. The adults introduce the activity by doing it themselves and then show the children what to do and do it with them.

Self-imposed restrictive routines

The routines that break up the day are imposed by the adults and provide a structure and are facilitating but others sometimes come from a child and are restrictive. These activities, to which a child compulsively returns, are not play. Some children are from homes where the domestic routine is repressive and they have an excessive and inappropriate need for order, tidiness and perfection and may fear doing something wrong or making a mistake. Direct help and support may be needed to lead them into a more flexible pattern, for example by the adults taking part in the activity. They show them that they find it safe, permissible and satisfying to experience and experiment. If they make a mistake or a mess, they acknowledge it and demonstrate that it can be put right, and if it cannot be put right, they verbalize their feelings and reassuringly put the difficulty into perspective.

The self-imposed, over-routinized behaviour of other children seems a defence. It protects their limited or precarious organization against the impact of an overwhelming and demanding world, but the security of the routine may remain a restricting need. The children are reassured because the adults acknowledge and protect their preoccupations and provide organization from without. They respond to the adults' help in loosening and extending their self-limiting personal routines, and find security within a broader classroom routine.

Protective rituals

The routines of some children are protective rituals that have a more obsessional and compulsive quality. They are intense preoccupations with a restricted, ritualized and sometimes bizarre routine. The children's involvement in the world about them is limited and they seem barely aware of the broader routine of the group. They seem lost in the content of their routine, rather than supported by its structure and sequence within the broader structure and sequence of the class routine, and if disturbed show great distress. Some of these children are at a nurture level of functioning, and their preoccupations seem to be non-productive symptoms rooted at the stage where purposeful growth had failed. The adults protect their preoccupations from the intrusion of other children, but take opportunities as they arise to extend and develop this obsessional activity in a more reality-directed way. They make a suggestion and introduce the necessary piece of equipment, or they involve themselves in the children's play as passive objects. In this way, they increasingly direct the energy that is locked up in these preoccupations into more normal, forward-moving interests.

Rituals of symbolic significance

The obsessional preoccupations of other children are within more complex experience and organization, and seem to have a more specific symbolic significance. Restorative nurture has only indirect relevance for problems of this kind. The fabric of nurture has become knotted, and nurturing experiences, which will strengthen a weak or loosely woven fabric, will not remove a tight knot. The children are nevertheless helped by the support that flows from a nurturing attitude and the attentive ear available for what are sometimes quite well articulated stresses and anxieties. The structure and pace of the group gives them 'space' to express unresolved problems, and constructive interests and relationships can be fostered at a more age-appropriate level.

Food

The intrinsic interest of food, and its importance in helping the children to give attention and to control their behaviour, has been considered in Chapter 4.

Food is a central feature of the parent–baby relationship, and the satisfaction and security inherent in early feeding become part of the child and support all later being and learning. It is important in the nurture groups because:

- it demonstrates caring, satisfies needs and provides basic learning experiences in many different ways
- for some children, it affirms the attachment for which they crave. For those who disregard the adult, it leads to an attachment because of the implicit control, and this control is the precursor of an attachment.

Children respond to food as it satisfies a common underlying need. Practitioners therefore use it to the full to gain and sustain the children's attention and the way they provide and use food is determined by the nature and extent of the children's early learning needs.

Food is experienced as caring

A group that is made up mainly of dependent, unhappy, inexperienced and poorly organized children who are fearful, fractious or angry needs affection, reassurance and encouragement, orderliness and organization, and support and help with controlled and directed nursery-level experiences. The children quickly respond to affection and attention, and form an attachment. They are essentially biddable children, though may not seem so at first, and when they have the security and satisfaction of the close proximity and attention of the adults in a situation appropriate for their needs, they are to some extent able to give attention, wait and share. Behaviour problems are usually manageable and the adults experience these as normal developmental difficulties, or an expression of distress. Food for these children is usually the 'family breakfast' at the table as described previously. It is a time of peace and relaxed, quiet satisfaction in a busy day full of new experiences; for many of the children, it seems to express the affection and attention they crave. It is a group occasion too and helps the children to relate to each other. Initially, they have little interaction, so having food together may at first be the only thing they are able to participate in and enjoy as a group. They are all doing and enjoying the same thing even though some may need help.

Food also provides a valuable link between home and school. Very few of the children sit down for their food at home, and 'family' food in school may be their first experience of this, and their first successful social interaction.

From the beginning, some groups seem like warm, intimate families where gentle and quiet insistence on controlled behaviour seems natural and normal. The children learn quickly and are proud of themselves. They take in that the adults are caring, and when they have internalized this caring, they begin to give and to do things for them and for each other. Food is then mainly an affirmation of a relationship that is being developed more widely and other satisfactions usually become more important to them.

'Breakfast': early learning content

The routine provision of food is however essential for children who are at a 'nurture' level. In most groups at the beginning of the year, irrespective of the nature of the children's difficulties, 'breakfast' early in the day is essential if the group includes children who actively resist forming an attachment and have severe behaviour problems. It is a routinized occasion and beforehand the children tidy up and wash their hands. This slows them down as well as contributing to a sense of personal worth.

The formality of the organization and ritual that is built into it reinforces early learning.

Preparation

When breakfast time comes, it is usual for the children to be collected in the home area. One adult sets the table. Later, the children take it in turns to help. Until the experience is secured, they are told what is to happen, what they have to do and what they are going to have. At this early stage, the food and the occasion itself is kept simple but it is presented formally and is at the table. As the children become more settled, the procedure becomes more flexible and complex and the teacher uses it for basic teaching; she might show pictures of the different items and they discuss what they will need and not need.

Explaining every step

The teacher tells them that they are going to have their drink and toast and explains step by step what they have to do, very slowly and in simple language that conveys one piece of information at a time, because they attend only to the first two or three words of a long complex sentence. The more impulsive children are likely to rush in so verbal restraints are built in as in any other activity: 'Sit quite still'; 'Wait until I say your name'. The most unrestrained children are likely to have been placed by the adults' feet and if necessary their hands are held. Every step is described and specified in detail.

The children are inexperienced and poorly organized. Some are not used to sitting to eat at a table, using knives and forks, or drinking from a cup or a beaker. The adults specify everyone and everything, and map out and organize the situation for each child in turn. One by one, they are sent off to the table in a considered order, each identified and acknowledged by name, and each in turn is directed to where to sit. It is usual for the most competent children to be sent off first. The others need the close proximity of an adult for as long as possible, and it is useful for them to see what the others do. Less secure or competent children might need extra support and help, a word of encouragement or a personal comment, given individually as they go off.

Giving individual help

The adult at the table receives each child individually, showing them where to sit. Care is taken to see that the children are seated comfortably. If necessary, they are helped to sit in the best position in relation to the table, for some of them are not only poorly coordinated but are poorly orientated to their surroundings, and have a poor sense of their own bodies in space. At this early stage, the adults decide where the children are to sit, for the situation is new to them. Even the more competent children may be uncertain of what is expected and may not know what to do, and without direction might choose one chair and then go to another, or would fight over them. They are therefore not allowed to choose where to sit. Later, when the adults know them better, they choose where they are to sit on the basis of likely compatibility. Later still, a free choice is given. Any children needing extra help are supported by one of the adults who explains exactly what they are to do; they check out that each child understands by asking them to repeat what has been said. A child who barely functions is reassured, and is told that there is a drink and toast for him, too. Another, who plunges unrestrainedly into everything, is told again, as often as necessary, what is expected.

Controls are built in

The meal is very carefully controlled, and it is usual when a group is new for the food to be kept out of sight until the children are sitting down and are still. The adults make positive requests, gently but with quiet insistence, if necessary to each child individually. At this stage, they control even minor fidgeting or posture which suggests that the children are not fully involved and attending. They quickly become biddable and are able to sit still if given something simple and specific to do. When incidental, undirected activity is controlled, the children are more likely to concentrate their attention fully on the adults, on the expected food and on the social requirements, which is the immediate aim. Later, when the children's behaviour is more constructive and purposeful, these requirements can be relaxed. In practice, this happens very soon.

Reinforcing the basic requirements

When the children are still, one adult fills each child's mug in turn. Children who are least able to wait are the first to get their drink, served individually, and are allowed to drink it straightaway provided they are sitting as required. Waiting is in this way made tolerable. More usually, the children are expected to wait until everyone is served. In a newly formed group, toast or biscuits would be offered only when all the children had finished their drink as they are unable to concentrate fully on more than one thing at a time. Delaying the food is, furthermore, a way of building in more waiting time. Gratification is delayed, expectation is heightened, and the motivation for controlled behaviour is increased. Grabbing is strictly controlled. At first, there is no choice; the children take the nearest piece and are not allowed to grab and those least able to wait get theirs first. They are allowed to eat it straightaway and holding back and waiting are gradually built up from there. Any child who can do little more than sit on the adult's lap and for whom the situation means nothing, is given 'privileged' treatment. No demands are made at first; delays and constraints are gradually introduced in a close parent–baby relationship. With reminders, most children are able to wait until all of them have their toast and then they are told they can begin. These imposed constraints are unnecessary if they are able to wait until everyone is ready.

The way food is managed is thus related to the social competence of the children and their tolerance for frustration, and the extent to which they can take in more than one thing at a time. But always the requirements are manageable and tolerable, and the satisfactions match the requirement and at every stage are considerable. Food is rarely withdrawn, though it might be held back until the children have settled again.

Most nurture children need to learn these basic social skills. Either they are inexperienced and without the self-control required, or are used to fending and fighting for themselves at home. Purposeful and controlled behaviour is usually soon established. The children quickly grasp that there is enough to go round and that they are included, and when they see what is required and realize that these requirements have to be met, they readily accept the constraints. In a few children, however, usually older ones, there is an aggressive and more deliberately purposeful aspect to their grabbing. They flaunt the constraints, size up the situation and see what is in it for them, and manipulate to get what they want or take what they want.

Progression

When the children are used to having food as a 'family' in school and can take in turn what is offered, verbal reminders to hold back are dropped. Instead, if a child still finds it difficult to wait, they might be asked to hand round the plate; this socially desirable behaviour gives satisfaction and replaces the more immediately gratifying but undesirable grabbing, and self-control is strengthened. Handing round the food becomes a special treat and is sought after. Gradually, the situation is fully in the children's hands; they are keenly aware of those who are behaving well, and when in charge are very strict and insist on 'please' and 'thank you'.

Enjoyment

When basic patterns of behaviour have been established, the children's attention is directed to eating properly, enjoying the food and the experience. At this stage, unnecessary restrictions can be relaxed. The children by now have some personal organization and self-control and their behaviour is no longer at the whim of immediate impulse. They are free within themselves to notice and enjoy what they are eating and take part in conversation. Initially inhibited children respond well to this approach. When shown what to do and that it is permissible, they can be encouraged to participate and to take, they get acknowledgement, appreciation and approval for making eye contact, and for taking the food. The children who at first uninhibitedly grab also learn from the others. They become aware of the needs of these children because in this slow-moving and controlled situation, there is time to take in what is happening.

Learning to make choices

Making choices is difficult for most of the children. Often, this is related to a paucity of earlier experiences, and limited internalization of the experiences and the memory of the feelings that went with them. Observations made by nurture group practitioners suggest that the children may appear to:

- be dead to experiences with no spontaneous impulse for doing or having anything
- be fragmented by anxiety, with too little identity to bring to the task of making a choice
- be fearful of committing themselves, or demonstrating that they exist by committing themselves; they are confused and distressed when expected to make a purposeful choice
- have a zest for experiences and have the agony of knowing that when they make a choice, they must forgo the things they have not chosen.

Whatever the nature of the children's indecision, in this slow-moving, quiet, orderly and controlled situation, the problems are verbalized, and they can be helped to choose. The choice arranged for them is at first very simple, perhaps between two kinds of jam to put on the toast. Each kind is on a separate plate because the children have become accustomed to taking the nearest and this principle would interfere with making a choice. The children have had both kinds on separate occasions, eaten slowly and with enjoyment. They remember each in imagery, and so are able to make a real choice. If a child dithers an uncomfortably long time, the adult relieves the distress by commenting on the alternatives, if necessary choosing for the child, by saying: 'I think you would like this one.' Making a choice is a considerable achievement for some of the children, and even though progress is carefully built up from simple to complex, immediate satisfaction to delayed satisfaction, they may have difficulty in accepting the consequences of their choice.

A girl who was offered the choice of a banana or raspberry milkshake chose the banana milk shake, but cried when it came because it was not pink. She was helped to cope with her distress and frustration because the adults shared the experience with her. They know how overwhelmingly disappointing and frustrating it is when a banana shake is not pink, and because they were emotionally close to her, they could put it all into words and help her through her feelings of distress. Soon the children learn to accept these disappointments. One teacher provided chocolate biscuits of different shapes. All the children had the major satisfaction of chocolate, but had to take the nearest biscuit and thus sacrifice the relatively minor satisfaction of the preferred shape.

Learning about one another

Watching a child learning to choose helps the others. They wait and watch with interest, knowing that their turn will come. A sense of identity and personal value is enhanced, the experience is heightened, and a spin-off is consolidation of self-control. In imagery, too, they share the choice and the struggle of the choice. In doing this, they begin to remember the foods the other

children like, and do not like. They get a picture of them as individuals, and begin to feel empathy as they identify with them.
Children watching in this way have a sense of providing support
and so feel supported when making a choice. They become more
aware of themselves as individual people who make choices, have
legitimate wants and are able to control them. The adults' comments indicate that they, too, remember what they like, respect
their tastes and treat them as valid, with the implicit acknowledgement that they are truly individuals, are valued and have
wants that are legitimately satisfied by others. All these things
contribute to a developing identity and maturity.

Situations like this are helpful also for unforthcoming children.
They begin to take part with more confidence when they see that
everything is orderly and everyone has a turn, and can be helped
to acknowledge and express their preferences. They may suddenly
refuse, often with passionate feeling, a jam they have accepted
daily without complaint, either not daring to say they didn't like
it, or not being sufficiently aware of themselves or the experience
to know that they don't like it. They learn to establish an identity
by realizing and saying that they don't like a particular jam. They
learn to make decisions and become, in the words of a teacher, 'a
proper person'. The pleasure the adults feel when a child takes the
first step in self-realization is tremendous, and there is often a
sense of exhilaration in the child.

Learning to share

Sharing, too, is important, and later the requirement to share is
deliberately introduced. There may be too few cakes to go round,
or one of the cakes is bigger and nicer than the others, and it is a
tremendous step for some of the children when they offer to
share. These expectations are built up very gradually so the children are able to tolerate them and learn from them. They are
helped by knowing that the adults are absolutely fair and often
give up nice things for them or go without.

Food occasions vary

As with families, food occasions are idiosyncratic and have their
own routine and ritual. As well as adding to the preparation time

and increasing expectation, they are in the collective ownership of the group, are personal to it and usually distinctive, and contribute to a group identity. Knives and forks are useful even if the food is simple, not only because they add to the ritual and the importance of the occasion, but because some of the children need help in using them. Cups and saucers are usual, though some groups have beakers. A few have drunk only from cups with feeding lips before coming to school, or from a feeding bottle, while others have had experience of cups or mugs but are clumsy. Straws are not recommended. Many of the children have very limited experience of different foods and so it is useful to introduce basic foods that are handled in different ways.

Involving the children

At the beginning, the adults prepare the food and the table and clear away. Soon the children are invited to help when they understand what is expected, and are sufficiently well organized and orderly to spread out the tablecloth and set the table. Later, they clear away and take their things to the sink. By the time the children have grasped the whole operation, the food is usually more varied and interesting. They are now capable of assisting in the preparation and do so in turn, while others help to clear away, wash up and put away. The adult is always there, showing them what to do, chatting with them and doing things with and for them, and is available to help when they want to do a job on their own and cannot quite manage. Everything is now more complex but a high level of organization is maintained, and although there is still a clear routine, this is more flexible in detail.

Helping to prepare the food

Helping to prepare the meal is very special for it is a shared and satisfying enjoyment in the context of a warm and friendly supportive family relationship. For some of them, it is a totally new experience. Others have heavy responsibilities at home. They carry these alone, often under stress and with considerable anxiety. In school, it is different. They enjoy watching the toast go brown with the adult close by, and talk without anxiety about the hazards of burning it, and they learn what the adult feels and does when it burns. Afterwards, they spread butter on the toast. All these are manageable responsibilities and are positive and happy experiences. When the food is ready, the children sit round the table with eagerness and enjoyment, and conduct themselves well. They have usually been shopping beforehand for the things they will need, and this makes the experience even more positive.

Helping to wash up

It is fun to help with the washing up because an adult is there and they chat together and laugh, and there is the special joy of immersing their hands in the bubbles in the sink and experiencing the feel of the bubbles. They blow them away and watch with the adult as they float away, break and disappear, exclaiming, enjoying, participating, making more and blowing harder ... gone! But this fun is under the control of the adults; they see that the washing up is done properly, from collecting and stacking to putting everything away in the right place. This, too, is an enjoyable experience. They all want to do the washing up and get pleasure from doing it all in an orderly way. Gradually, the children are able to do the washing up on their own, and this and other tasks, like folding the tablecloth, quickly become a treat and are sought after.

Sharing food encourages communication and language

In the early stages of a group, it is usual for the adults to make a running commentary on the food they are eating, for the children are not attuned to noticing and attending to their experiences, and their expressive language and basic vocabulary is extremely limited. If they are particularly unaware of themselves and their surroundings, one might comment on the shape of the biscuit: 'It's round and the plate is round', and the children take this up: 'I've got a round biscuit, I've got a round plate.' Or toast may be rectangular or a triangle and also crunchy. A very simple level of conversation is beginning to develop.

Very soon, everyone is more relaxed. The children know that the meal is part of the routine, and they know how they are expected to behave. They manage the food more naturally, talk about funny things that have happened in the group and laugh together. They become interested in the others, and their opinions, and begin to influence each other. The adults follow up and develop the comments the children make by referring to their own experiences. They make a point of talking about their homes and domestic things generally whenever an opportunity arises, but the breakfast table affords a particularly good opportunity for developing these personal themes. It becomes a natural 'Circle Time' (Mosley, 1996). In this situation, the children are responsive and are stimulated to talk, and remarkable conversational exchanges develop, and, because throughout the day their experiences are being extended, they gradually become interested in a wider range of things and have more to talk about.

Learning to listen and consider each other

Food within a family setting is also a means of fostering concentration and receptive language, for the children listen better to a story or an anecdote that is told, and in this context they get used to listening. It is the best situation of all in which to develop reciprocal, responsive and responsible attitudes. They learn to say 'please' and 'thank you'. These courtesies are a genuine acknowledgement of the person providing the food, and everyone in the group becomes associated with food and the good feelings that go with food.

Food carries a wide range of learning experiences

The food provided is trivial in relation to the experiences that are built in; as one assistant put it: 'We have a tremendous palaver for a tiny piece of toast.' The 'palaver' begins in the period immediately before the food when the children tidy away their things and wash their hands in the expectation of food. Tidying up and personal appearance are therefore suffused with the good feeling and positive attitude associated with food and with the adults' caring, and are experienced as pleasurable. In these circumstances, more than in most others, a positive attitude is likely to become internalized and self-motivating.

This is important because nurture group children typically have a poor self-image and poor personal organization. A positive attitude, deriving from the expectation of food, is perhaps later attached to the more formal attention-demanding tasks that in an established group immediately precede the food. Lastly, the formality, routine and control established at the breakfast table provide a structuring which persists for a considerable part of the morning, even in a newly formed group.

Further progression

When their basic emotional and social needs have been met, the children will often find other activities more attractive. Food then is offered only exceptionally, perhaps as a stabilizing comfort for children who are being tried in their mainstream class, or more routinely on Monday mornings if there are children whose home circumstances are particularly unstable and disturbing.

One adult might spontaneously suggest a meal, to evoke the experience they used to have and consolidate the feelings that went with it. Many groups decide to provide a little 'tea' at the end of the afternoon as this ends each school day with a sense of satisfaction and approval and is an acknowledgement of the effort that has gone before. It is an incentive to maintain high standards and gives a good start to the evening ahead.

When the children are more organized and can cope with a more complex and demanding exercise, some practitioners introduce a class lunch, either as a special occasion with invited guests or as a group event. The children help to plan and buy the food and prepare it, arrange the table, serve the food and wash up. Some groups have flowers on the table, and name cards; the name itself acknowledges the child's identity and presence and enhances their self-esteem. These occasions are a stimulus and provide interest, and reinforce a sense of personal well-being and of belonging to the group. They require considerable organization and control, and affirm their developing competence.

Birthday parties are always special occasions, but are introduced only when the children can cope. Most groups prepare special food. Some of the children do not know what birthdays are but they are always recognized in school and provide an opportunity for acknowledging the particular child, and having a party in which everyone shares. The birthday child chooses the menu, goes shopping with the assistant and a friend, and the other children buy or make cards. The child's friends from the mainstream class are often invited and the nurture children experience the pleasure of giving, and are proud to offer food and share their toys.

Some children are hungry

Some children, not necessarily those in the nurture group, come to school physically hungry; breakfast and out-of-school clubs now provide nourishing food to begin the day. Breakfast in the nurture group may continue on an optional basis with other needy children from the school coming in to make a specially formed family group.

Feeding difficulties

Some of the children have eating difficulties of many different kinds; they include picking at food, food fads, fearing to eat, gobbling and choking, failure to chew and swallow, indiscriminate eating of anything at hand, and squeezing the food or crumbling it. Some refuse to eat unless fed and a small number still have a bottle at home and are unable to feed themselves. In this relaxed slow-moving setting, they can be given small amounts of food selected for them at first, and can be helped step by step to eat more normally. Occasionally, a child is hungry and providing food comes before learning to wait and not grab.

Practitioners are aware of and sensitive to religious and cultural requirements and will find opportunities for providing and sharing food from other traditions.

Baking

Baking is an important activity in the nurture groups which is introduced as soon as the children are sufficiently well organized and coordinated to cope. It is kept very simple, and at first the children might do no more than stir the mix, and watch as the adult eases the cakes or pizza onto the cooling rack. As they progress, they begin to help at every stage, and in time are able to manage a sequence of steps on their own, and later in the day they share what has been cooked. In some groups, the children whose turn it is to bake take some of the food home or parents are invited to share it. This is usually a good experience, for even those parents who initially feel critical of the activities in the nurture group recognize that this is an achievement, and value their children for this. The children's self-esteem is enhanced and because they are giving something of themselves to their parents, the parents feel proud too.

More imaginative baking is possible later and may be extended out into the school, perhaps making cakes to share with other classes for a special occasion. Later still, it is sometimes possible, with careful planning, to invite the children from a neighbouring nurture group for a party. Festivals give scope for food from different faith traditions to be baked. In some schools, these festivals are whole-school events and may be part of international days or evenings, with parents, siblings and other guests such as school governors, invited. Some groups have parents' parties and the children help to write the invitations and prepare the food.

Picnics, too, can be special occasions. The group shops for the food and prepares it together, they think through what they need to take with them, and the best way of packing and carrying the food.

Summary □

- Children and young people in nurture groups need opportunities to relive the missed experiences from early childhood within a parent–child relationship. For some, this may be at the earliest baby level and opportunities may need to be provided for older children through drama and role play.

- Communication, language and play develop through clearly recognizable stages when the resources are available and the adults interact and model for the children.

- Food is central to the parent–child relationship and therefore is an essential feature of nurture groups. It demonstrates caring and provides many basic learning experiences.

Further reading

Benner, G.J., Nelson, J.R. and Epstein, M.H. (2002) 'Summary of Language Skills of Children with EBD: A Literature Review', *Journal of Emotional and Behavioural Disorders*. Available at: www.literacytrust.org.uk [accessed 10 July 2009]. Communication and language are vital for children's development and learning. Missed early stages are often the cause of behaviour difficulties later.

Bruce, T. (1996) *Helping Young Children to Play*. London: Hodder and Stoughton. This book looks at the developmental stages of play.

DCSF (2008) *Every Child a Talker: Guidance for Early Language Lead Practitioners*. Available at: www.nationalstrategies.gov.uk [accessed 22 September 2009]. These materials produced in response to the Bercow Inquiry by the Royal College of Speech and Language Therapists (www.rcslt.org) and EYFS Communication, Language and Literacy provide a good guide to the developmental stages and practical suggestions for teaching.

Sonnet, H. (2008) *Nurturing Success: How to Create and Run an Effective Nurture Group*. Wisbech: LDA. This book describes current practice in nurture groups.

Becoming Independent Learners

This chapter explores the cognitive strands within earliest learning and how these shape an inclusive curriculum. Nurture group practitioners provide children and young people with:

- a holistic learning experience of intermeshing emotional, social and cognitive developmental strands that cannot be separated out
- emotional and cognitive experiences that with continuing support lead to self-awareness, self-regard, a positive self-image and empathy with others
- a positive attitude to others and an enthusiasm to experience and explore and solve problems
- the dispositions and the sense that someone has faith in them which motivate them to achieve, and which are intimately a part of early cognitive growth and later independent learning.

Children and young people in nurture groups lack trust in people and events, have a poor self-image and are without constructive purpose. They fear failure and may even fear to function, and for some the response of the adults to their achievements means as much or even more than the achievement itself, so great is their need to be valued. Their limited cognitive competence is bound into a general impairment of early developmental learning opportunities.

Nurture group practitioners build in the foundations for cognitive growth at the same time as they meet the social and emotional needs at the earliest level.

An inclusive curriculum

The experiences that establish attachment and trust also have cognitive content which is the earliest level of an inclusive curriculum; it familiarizes the children with themselves and the world and people immediately about them. They become better organized, and gain mastery of simple skills and some understanding of process in the world.

The curriculum, pedagogy and provision for Special Educational Needs (SEN) have undergone dramatic developments since the first nurture groups were set up 40 years ago.

> The Nurture Group model emphasized the children's capacity for growth and for learning, but perhaps inevitably the first priority in that period [1970s] was to evolve effective strategies for addressing their emotional and social needs. With hindsight, it is possible to recognize that many of the features of the approach are characteristic of what is now most highly valued in strategies for educational inclusion.
>
> (Cline, 2006 in Lucas et al., 2006: 3).

Nurture groups meet the requirements for inclusion (DfES, 2001a) and the National Curriculum principles for inclusion (DfEE/QCA, 1999: 30). How nurture groups do this is described in detail in *Nurture Group Principles and Curriculum Guidelines: Helping Children to Achieve* (Lucas et al., 2006). The principles of inclusion require children to experience the (now extended) curriculum at the level they are at, rather than according to their chronological age. While social and emotional learning take priority in the nurture group, entitlement to the National Curriculum is crucial (DfES, 2001a).

Working with other agencies

Nurture groups have always worked with other professionals (CCETSW, 1978; Bennathan and Boxall, 2000). The Children Act

2004 requires local authorities to have a unified approach to children's services. Other disciplines such as educational psychology, social services, child and adolescent mental health services (CAMHS), occupational therapy, speech and language therapists and physiotherapy as well as specialist teachers have expertise to support individual children with specific difficulties or for group work. Some children in nurture groups may be diagnosed with other special needs requiring specialist input. A far greater range of SEN are now found in nurture groups. Research suggests that these children may benefit from nurture group provision (Cooper, 2002), however as they might not be able to reintegrate into a mainstream class, they are not nurture children in the strict sense despite having nurture needs, and other SEN provision may be more appropriate once these nurture needs have been met. A staff and leadership team, confident in the nurture group approach, will determine their level of involvement with other agencies and ensure that the support is in sympathy with its ethos and enhances the nurture curriculum.

The nurture curriculum

Whether spontaneous or planned, the teacher builds in directed, constrained and focused work from the beginning, by purposefully developing the learning possibilities of experiences and situations as they arise, at the developmental level the child has reached. The nurture curriculum is explicit teaching at the earliest level for those children described as 'nurture children' (see Chapters 1 and 10). Even KS2 children may not manage one-to-one correspondence when they count or be able to manage simple counting games. They need help with these activities, and are not being resistive when they do not engage with them. This earliest level of teaching follows that of the parent with a normally developing younger child. The objectives are the same but the circumstances are not, and the process is more complex than in the early years. The centrally (DCSF) provided curriculum materials available to schools to support inclusion are a valuable resource for both the nurture and the nurturing curriculum.

A multi-sensory approach

There is a high incidence of perceptual and motor coordination difficulties in children in the nurture groups. Attention to these is a priority and takes the form of structured, multi-sensory activities centring on listening and looking, discriminating and remembering (see Chapter 6).

Learning to attend and think

Purposeful attention-giving and motivation underpin the skills, language and concepts normally gained in the first three years and are an essential part of the nurture curriculum. They come through the close relationship of adult and child; and are integral to the EYFS and its supporting materials and to the National Curriculum.

Nurture group practitioners facilitate children's cognitive development by extending their awareness, as parents would, through spontaneous involvement in and through early years level play and experiences and, where appropriate, through National Curriculum-related activities.

The learning content in the structure of the day

The organization and structuring of a nurture group day is an attempt to re-create the conditions of the early childhood (0–3) years, and within this to provide a saturation of developmentally relevant experiences. The adults help the children to give attention by verbalizing in detail objects, events and expectations. They maintain routines, clear time intervals, sequence and order, stress looking, listening and recall, and provide the repetition needed to establish and consolidate the experience. All this contributes to the ordered acquisition of skills and concepts, enriched by the adults in language, and strengthened because they are personally involved with the children, share their experiences and give support and purposeful direction. They gain a sense of relationships in space and time and events in relation to each other, and in the course of this a sense of their own identity, of themselves in relation to the world and as an agent of change. And in experi-

menting with change, they begin to grasp cause-and-effect relationships.

The organization, conduct and content of the day: its relevance to cognitive growth

Some of the learning inherent in the children's experiences in the
nurture group derives directly from the organization and conduct of
the day, some from the experiences within this structure. Below are
examples of the structure and content intrinsic to the children's day
that are of immediate and direct relevance to cognitive growth.

Routines:	provide security, identity, delineate the day and contribute to a sense of time.
Lining up:	allows children to gain a sense of discrete units and order.
Selecting their name/ photograph card:	provides a meaningful introduction to symbolic representation.
Finding the right pocket for their card:	focuses on one-to-one (1:1) correspondence, left to right order and a notion of categories.
Establishing the day and the month:	gives the experience of number, sequence and category, and contributes to a sense of time.
Action songs and games:	provide organization, rhythm and pattern.
Giving news; talking about yesterday's events:	focuses on recall, verbalization and the ordering of ideas.
Carpet time talk and activities:	extends vocabulary and helps build up basic concepts, and a sense of periods of time.

Underlying everything is the focus on attention-giving which is
the primary precondition of learning.

Earliest learning experiences

The interests and experiences of babies and young children are
intrinsically bound into their physical growth, and in particular

their mobility and physiological rhythm. Sensitive parents intuitively provide an appropriate environment and relate in a developmentally relevant way, and, without special planning on their part, the young child's growth follows a hierarchically developing pattern of increasingly complex organization.

Older nurture group children and young people have the same early developmental needs but are physically more advanced. Their experiences will more often be curriculum-led. The nurture teacher assesses their developmental needs using the Boxall Profile and National Curriculum attainment levels or P scales, sets manageable targets and looks at how they can be achieved. The learning experiences involved have developmental content equivalent to that of the early childhood years. They may be different in form, and an activity or situation may have different developmental content for different children and satisfy needs at different levels for any one individual.

> Maria, aged 9, enjoyed helping in the garden. She had planted some sunflower seeds with one of the adults and was assiduous in watering and caring for the garden. Some time later, she was found in the garden digging up the seeds to see if they had started to grow.

Teacher-extended learning

The nurture group provides developmentally appropriate experiences equivalent to those normally gained in early childhood (see Chapter 1 – Earliest learning: a summary chart, p. 7). Some experiences may recapture not only an awareness of warmth, softness, comfort and movement but also a passive experience of simple sequencing as the adult plays 'this little piggy ... '. The cognitive content hinges on the close involvement in action and language between the adults and individual children and is intuitively structured, as with parents, in accordance with their developmental needs. The adults support these experiences in language, so developing them incidentally but purposefully. Choosing the right clothes for the doll involves concepts of relative size; the fun of wearing a shawl in dressing-up play can lead into verbal concepts of length and size, and then measurement and area. These different activities are part of the nurture group day. They satisfy an emotional need and engage and hold the children's attention, are enjoyable and further their personal and social development, and, because they engage and hold the children's attention, are enjoyable and satisfy an emotional need – they are an important vehicle for cognitive development.

Basic concepts in everyday experiences

Replicating early childhood offers opportunities such as incidental counting as they jump up the steps of the school as though with a parent, or put spoons alongside bowls of cereal with an adult nearby. Other experiences are more complex and elaborate. When preparing breakfast, the children learn where items are kept, that certain things are stored together because they are linked by function or by size, and are classified in that way. Visual prompts on the cupboard doors are an indication of the contents of the cupboard and are another experience of symbolic representation.

These operations, including other typical early cognitive activities of the EYFS, require skill in coordinating movements, visuo-spatial judgement and experience of orderliness and one-to-one correspondence. Helping with these tasks is particularly satisfying because they are associated with food and enhance self-esteem; any anxiety is manageable because the adult is there to support and share the problems and the pleasure. The situation is therefore one in which learning is at a high level. Breakfast, in particular, provides opportunities to develop concepts of volume and size, subtraction and division, addition and multiplication. After breakfast, they wash up, stacking according to size, recall where the different things go and put them away in an orderly fashion. In the course of this, there are many opportunities for matching, ordering, sequencing and categorizing, and basic, practical mathematics.

Everyday domestic activity

Early learning happens through regular, repeated activity and early years teachers plan for opportunities to cook, garden, shop, wash up, do laundry work, cleaning and sweeping, all important in the development of cognition, but missed by nurture children because of their lack of engagement and unmet social and emotional needs. All these activities involve development of language, fine and gross motor coordination skills, sensory awareness, sequencing and ordering, connecting ideas, cause and effect, and the nature of change (Gopnik, 2009). Food is especially important, partly because it is a basic need.

The children enjoy cooking; it is rich in learning experiences and simply making toast under a grill can have important learning content.

> Simon had been very disruptive in the nursery; he interfered continually in other children's play and never settled to an activity without adult support.
>
> For the first few weeks in the nurture group, he challenged the adults constantly, grabbing at everything. Gradually, he began to be able to wait a little longer for his toast but always wanted to sit where he could watch it being made under the grill. One day, he gave a great sigh. When asked why, he was able to say that he understood now that the grill had browned it – it had not been coloured with a crayon.

The opportunities for the development of skills, concepts and language are considerable, whatever the level of the children, and learning is maximized because of the fundamental importance and interest of food and cooking in purely personal terms, and the anticipation of something nice to eat at the end.

Using 'real' things is vital because the basic life experience of many of the children is inadequate and their concepts are vague and poorly developed, or even false.

Communication and language

The nature and structure of the language spontaneously used by the adults in these everyday domestic activities is evoked by their close identification and involvement with individual children and is an integral and reciprocal part of the nurturing relationship. In emotional content and cognitive style, it is relevant to the stage they have reached and so consolidates their development. At the same time, it leads them forward, providing direction and a sense of purpose. At an early level, it helps foster a sense of well-being and positive self-image, and later as it progresses and changes, it engenders in the children a sense of themselves as achieving and moral individuals. In all these ways, it is of profound importance and in the nurture group the adults verbalize everything throughout the day. Language is also vital in shaping the development of concepts and thinking skills through description and comment on situations and behaviour; it extends children's experiences beyond the immediate situation, thus creating a wider conceptual context in which awareness and understanding can be developed, and generalizations made.

Shaping language

The adults share all basic experiences with the children and in a running commentary describe qualities, draw out similarities and comment on differences. Together, they recall what has happened in the group and in the stories they have heard, and they have games of 'What does this do?' and 'What is this for?' The past experience of the children is so limited that the adults rarely attempt to draw observations from them at this stage but instead provide a great deal of information. For a long time, too, they avoid direct questions, but indirectly ask a question of themselves, and answer it: 'Let's do this … I wonder what will happen? Oh, look, it's … ', or they accept a fragment from the child and develop it into an idea for them, as parents would with a younger child. 'Why?' questions are rarely appropriate; they presuppose an advanced level of understanding and the maturity to reflect on an experience or process and analyse it, and are often experienced as a threat or taken as an attack, especially by older children. Parents in a developmentally comparable situation would not distance children in this way and leave them exposed to failure, but would verbally re-create the situation, bring it to life and share the problem. Concrete examples and demonstration make meanings absolutely clear and just as the normally developing young child spontaneously echoes what is said, the adult often asks the child to repeat back what has been said. This focuses the attention of a less experienced child on the sounds, and directs the attention of others to the content. This is important, because the attention of many of the children is poorly sustained, and they sometimes pick up a fragment only and incorporate this into an existing imperfect or distorted concept, often by association rather than logical connection.

Speaking and listening

Most of the children when they come into the group have very poor language skills (see Chapter 6). Encouraging them to talk coherently, and to listen to each other and develop conversation, is an important part of the work of the group. Valuable opportunities arise in the home area around the family table or in incidental talk with the adults. Some of the most productive conversations develop on visits to the local shops or the park, or on their journeys further afield. Later on, the adults frequently remind them of the things they have done together at these times: 'Do you remember ... ?' At first, most of the children have little or nothing to talk about, but as their interest is engaged and their experience widens, they become more aware of and interested in each other and talk together about the things they have heard in stories, and begin to ask interested questions. Photographs taken in class or on visits evoke lively observations, reinforce personal and group identity and provide material for their personal and class storybooks, written with the teacher's help.

Modelling

Many of the children love more than anything else to listen as the adults talk together about their homes and their domestic lives, modelling conversation (DfEE, 1998: 8). They eagerly ask what their children have done and whether they have been naughty, what they have had to eat, and how many pairs of shoes they have. The adults make a point of enquiring about each other's families, showing interest and concern. They talk about the food they cook at home, and draw from the children comments about *their* food at home. The children become absorbed in these personal stories. They learn a great deal from them and ask for the same anecdote over and over again with all the details. As they listen to their domestic talk, they begin to build up a picture of the adults; they become real people to them, with real families, living in real houses and flats, and they feel closer to them. Not all these conversations are of immediate interest to the children, but they help to fill in vast empty areas in their experience and provide links with their own lives, and the children begin to take these up and conversations develop.

Sharing stories and reading

The children need individual storytime, opportunities to read together as well as individually and a time to listen to stories as a group. During individual storytime, it is natural for the adult to put an arm round the child. The more immature children seem to be taking in the warmth of the adult and the music of their voice rather than the story itself. Individual storytime has a very special closeness, but other children nearby become absorbed and several might draw near. The most dependent children sit closest to the adult while others listen from a distance while doing something else. All at some time like to be very close, and to be read to. For all of them, their own special time with the adult is very important.

The adult introduces the children to reading individually or in twos or threes. The context is relaxed, and affection and approval are evident. All are absorbed in the story and there is a pleasurable feeling of closeness with the adult. The children spontaneously comment and ask questions, and those who otherwise show no interest in books snuggle in and turn their heads to look at the page.

Group storytime is more formal; children sit on the carpet or, if older, on chairs or cushions in front of the adult. Most quickly give their full attention to the story and become totally absorbed. Simple, well-structured stories with good, clear illustrations can be read many times because the children usually have a poor attention span. A favourite story with a nurturing theme can be the prompt for a range of other activities (see Figure 2). Older children may enjoy a longer book read as a serial or one with direct language but high interest content suitable for KS2 and 3. Aspects of the English curriculum may arise incidentally but focused teaching should not detract from the experience of engaging with the story.

The importance of the attachment relationship

The experiences that arise during the course of the nurture group day are thus at many different levels. Some directly reflect the attachment relationship and the child is 'lost' in the closeness, peace and security. Other experiences and the language that is part of them have more cognitive content, but they too are bound into an attachment relationship. The cognitive content is therefore part of the nurturing experience; it is fostered and developed largely intuitively and has direct implications for cognitive growth leading to independent learning. Both adults share this responsibility; it does not derive solely from the teacher's professional qualifications.

The National Curriculum

The nurture group teacher, with the assistant and in collaboration with the mainstream class teacher, is also responsible for ensuring the child's entitlement to the knowledge, skills and understanding of the National Curriculum. These are incremental and children work at their appropriate level (DfEE/QCA, 1999: 30). Some children, those described as 'children who need nurturing' (see Chapters 1 and 10), may need to work at an earlier Key Stage in some subjects but will be capable of age-appropriate work in others.

The nurturing curriculum

Many of the children are potentially able and want to succeed in school and their frustration and profound sense of failure are often factors in their behaviour difficulties. Formal curriculum work will most often be the nurturing curriculum, that is, missed work from an earlier level or Key Stage of the National Curriculum including EYFS. These skills and concepts are essential for progress

Visual

- Use puzzles, picture pairs, models and props
- Match and identify different materials and suit patterns
- Draw own suit for merging into background
- Make suits to act out story
- Closely observe the book – ask/answer questions
- Sequence and sort the story using suit props
- Try games like feelings bingo, turn-taking, sharing

Lesson Plan: Halibut Jackson by David Lucas (2003)

Auditory

- Read story aloud, or try paired reading
- Listen to story on tape/CD
- Use different music for each scene
- Tell the story using musical instruments for Halibut in each setting
- Practise different ways of walking, making a noise – quietly/stamping/shuffling – would Halibut make a noise?
- Sing songs related to Halibut's adventures – fruit/food, quietness

Tactile/Kinaesthetic

- Utilise drama and role play, dressing in different fabrics/materials/clothes to blend in with background
- Make play dough/clay/junk models of buildings
- Construct scenes within a shoe box and hide Halibut
- Make Halibut with 2/3 different outfits
- Make Halibut and collage him with material like one of the suits from the book
- Compare and contrast as many fabrics as possible, e.g. wool/cotton/silk/satin, etc.

This is a simple multi-sensory activities plan relating to a book read and enjoyed by a nurture group

Figure 2. The Halibut Plan

in the National Curriculum. Their acquisition is of great importance because:

- lack of basic competence causes frustration, and this may lead to outbursts of temper, inconsequential behaviour, avoidance or listlessness, as well as being damaging to children's self-esteem
- when an integrated skill is built up, children gain a sense of organization, orderliness and sequence, and the pleasure of achievement
- they internalize these complex activities, experience them in imagery, and can therefore anticipate the effects of their actions and so modify their intentions. They learn to think before they act
- mastery of these skills meets a developmental need and so children are motivated to give considerable attention to the task. This creates a disposition to concentrate, and cumulatively developing interests are opened up
- their experiences with adults help establish contentment, closeness and shared satisfaction. They feel secure and contained, and are responsive. Motivation and involvement in the task increase and attachment is strengthened
- acquiring a basic competence increases the possibility of constructive interaction with the other children and enhances self-esteem.

The task of the adults in developing the children's competence is threefold:

1. they engage and sustain their interest and attention by providing relevant experiences at an appropriate level
2. they help them differentiate and organize these experiences
3. they build on this competence in the hierarchical development of skills and concepts.

A great deal of individual work is necessary. Unlike normally developing younger children, many show little interest and spontaneous involvement in the things about them, and even when engaged at an appropriate level, their attention is rarely sustained. Others are greedy for experiences but cannot use them. It is therefore important, no matter what their age, to build up a repertoire of games and activities that carry the learning experiences normally gained in the earlier years. Some of these activities also provide an outlet for energy. They become familiar to the children, capture their interest and attention, and through them they learn to look, listen and give attention, and as they experiment and explore, they begin to connect up different aspects of their experience.

These early experiences are essential prerequisites of the ability to reconstruct in imagery and language, and so lead on to problem-solving.

Sensory and motor experience

The teacher often observes basic deficits in early-level competencies during the course of directed group activities, or when children are being introduced individually to a new toy or task. They may have difficulty in indicating body parts, have poor directional hand control or fine motor coordination and so time is given to developing body image, perception of spatial relationships and hand–eye coordination on an individual basis. Many of the games played in the home area draw on basic experiences that school-age children are assumed to have, but quite often reveal unexpected difficulties. Thus, when required to guess by feel what is hidden in the 'feely bag', they may fail to identify the object by touch because they have not had adequate prior experience of seeing and feeling each object on its own.

Objects of different size, texture and resistance to touch were spread out on a large plain-coloured square cloth, and the teacher described their qualities. The children looked at them, touched them, felt and explored them, shook and banged them, and the teacher made a running commentary. Specially designed felt masks that were acceptable to the children were used as blindfolds. They felt and tried to describe and identify the object placed in their hands. At first, the others called out, but very soon they learned to contain their eagerness, and to wait for their turn.

Visuo-motor coordination difficulties

Many nurture group children are poorly coordinated in their gross movements; they bump into things and people, and knock them over. Motor coordination difficulties are apparent when the children try to dress themselves, or play simple games in PE. Simple activities such as throwing and catching, hand-clapping, holding hands and hopping together on one foot or lifting one or other leg on request help them to develop a more valid body image and to manage their bodies in space.

> Passing a bean bag round the circle requires practice because it involves watching, taking, holding and passing on, all difficult operations for inexperienced children. In one school, when two bean bags were passed round, the children continued to watch the progress of the first bag instead of turning to wait for the second one. Passing a ball between their legs or over their heads to another child also presented problems because they did not let go until they could see the other child.

Coordinating two simultaneous tasks, for example walking upstairs while holding a plate, can be difficult. They need help with balance, movement and directed action; verbal instructions of up, down, forwards and backwards, which are directly linked with the actions, lead to an internalized sense of spatial relationships.

Many of the children who have poor control of their own movements and of themselves in relation to the objects around them also have a poor sense of volume and quantity, and little idea of what is practicable. They may have difficulty in carrying a full jug, and need an adult to be there to watch them, and to tell them to go slowly and carefully. Even older children may have difficulty with simple tasks of this kind and need help at every stage.

Some children have difficulty with fine visuo-motor coordination, evident when they try to button their clothes, or their hands are limp and movements poorly directed. Finger movement practice, such as digging their hands into dough to make patterns, is helpful.

Listening, attending and remembering

Many activities in the home area already mentioned encourage learning to listen and pay attention to sounds. For example:

- identifying, locating and imitating sounds of differing kinds
- games of discriminating between sounds
- concepts of same, different, loud, soft, first, last and in the middle
- rhythmic patterns, tapped out, lend themselves to games of remembering, copying and discriminating
- elaborating, e.g. the child whose name pattern is clapped out is asked to get the biscuits
- verbal memory games, which also foster listening and remembering: the children pick out items specified by name from a collection of small objects presented afterwards, or they 'play' at following simple instructions. Functions of objects can be built in later
- action songs and singing games are important at all ages; children attend to the sounds and become more aware of sounds and rhythms; they learn the names of parts of the body, the use of prepositions, and in linking words with actions gain a better sense of body image.

Many of the children have speech problems of varied kinds and origin, including poor production and enunciation of words, and these games are helpful, both directly and indirectly. They contribute to a sense of self because of their direct focus on the person of the child, turn-taking enables them to begin to listen to each other and a personal interest develops. Recording and playback can be helpful.

Looking and remembering

Other games in the home area centre around paying attention to the things they see and remembering them – for example, identifying objects on a tray, naming and describing them and recalling what is missing when one is taken away; guessing what is being described – 'I am thinking of … ', matching the doll's house furniture or the animals to pictures on cards and when they are put into the 'feely bag', they find by touch the one represented on the card the teacher holds up.

Forming basic concepts

A great deal of work on basic concepts develops from experiences within the nurturing relationship. Everyday domestic items are a natural vehicle for early concept development but resources from EYFS or KS1 may be useful for sorting, grouping and ordering according to size, shape, colour, function, families, pairs; picture cards for sequencing, action cards, pictures of objects that make familiar noises, card games involving listening and looking and then formulating an answer or making a decision; as well as dolls' houses, villages, railway sets and so on. Coloured shapes can be used for matching and grouping and sequencing by shape and colour, and later for copying patterns or following instructions to work in a particular way. Children gain much-needed experience of fine motor control and coordination through these activities and persistence as the pieces are put together. And, for all of them, they are the basis of verbally formulated mathematical concepts, developed individually.

Play and creativity

Creative activities in nurture groups are similar to those in mainstream classes, but are weighted to an earlier level of experience and learning (see Chapter 6). Creativity begins with sensory exploration whatever the age of the child. Music, for example, is for some children the exuberant pleasure of being the agent of a great big noise. For others, it involves taking turns or the learning may lie in stopping and starting, making loud and soft sounds or following a pattern. Finger-painting, hand and foot printing, role play, drama and dance are enjoyable and motivating; they contribute to body image and self-awareness and require control and this is gradually built up. Children need time to explore and respond using all their senses.

Adults must themselves value creativity and be involved as well as providing ideas, creating images, highlighting feelings, and leading the children into new understandings and awareness by their interjections; they give direct support, share the experience and participate in the activity as an equal partner to a greater extent than in the mainstream class. Appreciation of children's efforts is also directed more to the growing edge of the individual's developing skills, for example for holding an instrument or the scissors well or showing initiative, than to the end product, though this, too, would elicit pleasure.

> For some nurture children, creative work contributes to their first awakenings of physical self-awareness. A child in a KS2 group saw himself for the first time when he looked in the classroom mirror, and another child who was painting in an outline of himself, coloured brown only the parts he could see, gradually extending this as he pushed up his sleeves to see more.

Cross-curricular themes and linked work

Themes may be planned for the nurture group or linked to work in a child's mainstream class and involve all areas of learning, for example people who care for us, transport etc. The children draw on direct experience and from stories read to them. All involve thinking through what is required, planning in discussion, and finding, making and organizing the necessary equipment; cooperation and sharing; and giving and accepting roles, active and passive. Hospitals involve making and accepting physical contact, which many of them find difficult, caring for each other and physical awareness. When playing hospitals, they find and name body parts – also difficult for many of the children. At the hairdressers, they cut out pictures of hairstyles and make magazines for the customer to read. They become aware of their appearance as they discuss styles and care of the hair, and with this comes self-esteem, and indirect eye contact as the customer and stylist look at each other in the mirror. The learning opportunities are at different levels and are immense; role play can develop imaginatively and sometimes has therapeutic content.

Managing the nurturing curriculum

Directed work can be a respite for the children as it provides organization and direction rather than requiring it. Formal work, therefore, is stabilizing, provided it is at the appropriate level and is likely to fit into their expectations of school and those of parents. The aim is to get the children to the stage when they can constructively use the wide range of experiences and relationships of the mainstream class and can engage with the National Curriculum at their own level. To achieve this, they need formal attainments and the personal resources for adequate participation in age-appropriate activities. Stress is therefore placed from the beginning on acquiring the basic literacy and numeracy skills and the widening of experiences, and through this the development of concepts in order to close the gap between the children's achievements and the expectations of the mainstream class teacher.

Formal work is built into the routine from the beginning. Most of the children, however, function constructively only within an early and close 'parent–child' relationship. Even when they seem able to manage an activity on their own, they may need the pleasure, reassurance and security of doing things with the adult. Their response to the homely running commentary that accompanies this is not necessarily because they need this level of language but because they need the more intimate relationship of which it is a part. KS2 and 3 children will accept and use a close relationship of this kind when they are secure within the group. Formal work is therefore in the context of a more intimately supportive relationship than is usual in the mainstream class and there is the same attention to detail and individual need as described earlier (see Chapters 3 and 4).

Differentiation and individual learning plans

The level of development catered for in different groups and within a group varies considerably and planning will need to be carefully differentiated, individual and personalized according to effective SEN practice. Again, it is the quality and nature of the relationships with the adults that is vital and no matter what the level of competence of the children, the adults watch over them and intervene and give active help to any child who seems confused. They anticipate anything that might go wrong, because most of the children have a low tolerance for frustration and might express this in destructive action.

Protected work space

As children in nurture groups have a poor tolerance for real or imagined interference by others, it is particularly important that they are well spaced. Sometimes formal work is staggered through-out the day and two or three children at the most are at the work table at any one time, spaced to avoid accidental nudging or inter-ference. Larger group tables, intended for collaborative work, encourage a high level of peer group interaction but for nurture group children, they are a source of distraction and interference. Collaboration requires considerable personal organization and self-control, and a high level of motivation for the task in hand, not characteristics of 'nurture' children.

Pace

National Curriculum work proceeds as it would in the mainstream class, but at a slower pace, with a focus on early skills and listening experiences, and a great deal of direct support, encouragement, reas-surance and praise, and detailed verbalization. More repetition is needed, partly because the children are mastering unfamiliar tasks and are coordinating skills that normally would have been well prac-tised at an earlier stage, but also because they need the pleasure of anticipated success, and the satisfaction of the reality of success. It is important that the activity gives a visually gratifying end result, but above all else it is essential that the requirements are realistic and commensurate with the child's developmental level. Pressure to achieve at this level is considerable and good standards are expected, but at the same time high expectations for the future are maintained. It is not easy at first to tune in to an early enough level and to work unhurriedly at this level when there is so much ground to make up, but in time there is progression and extended writing and higher-level mathematical understanding is possible.

Growth towards personal and social autonomy

Nurture children are not confined to the nurture classroom; they are within and part of the school, and are exposed to complex and changing events and reactions of other people over which the nurture teacher may have little control. These situations need to be planned for, and including nurture provision in whole-school policies is essential. Assembly, lunchtime and playtime are major areas of potential difficulty, as are off-site visits and celebrations. Detailed planning and imagination in anticipating possible hazards are necessary as well as undertaking risk assessments.

Assembly, lunchtime and playtime demand considerable personal organization and self-control, and for nurture children present particular difficulty. They are thrust into the close proximity of large numbers of unfamiliar children in a big space that has no immediately visible limits. The structure and routine may be unfamiliar, the situation bewildering and they are without the direct, immediate and personal support and control of an adult with whom they have a special relationship. Situations of these kinds are likely to exacerbate problems and may generate them.

Assembly

Assembly usually presents less difficulty than lunchtime or playtime. Assembly itself is a ritualized event which is repeated day after day and has form and familiarity. All present are required to engage with the ritual and behave appropriately, including other adults present, who model the expectation, for example of listening to music as everyone comes in. The children need to be prepared for assembly in a relaxed way with reminders about the behaviour that is expected.

In a small school where nurture group children's needs are understood, it is usually possible for most of them, given adequate preparation and support, to participate from the beginning. A very inexperienced, unorganized child for whom the situation was meaningless would not be able to manage alone and might need direct support or a soft toy. More usually, such children do not go to a whole-school assembly; they are taken in only when they have a concept of the larger school group. Children who are developmentally a little more advanced may be able to manage if they are close to an adult.

Contributing to an assembly is recognition that the children are part of the larger school community, and the extent to which they are expected to take part must take their needs into account and the nurture teacher's immediate aims for the group must be a consideration. Participation at whole-school level is rarely feasible at the beginning. Some children barely function at first, even in the nurture group. For others, a public display is likely to exacerbate showing off and could lead to uncontrolled excitement and tantrums, while for those who have serious problems of self-regard, it is a situation of embarrassment and humiliation. Other children thrive when the centre of attention and gain from the experience, provided they are carefully prepared and closely monitored. In spite of the difficulties, most nurture groups are able to contribute something of interest if required, if the context is sympathetic. A nurturing school, primary or secondary, will often use assemblies to reinforce 'nurturing' themes of their own or SEAL resources.

Lunchtime

Lunchtime may be more difficult; for all the children in the school, it is a time of physical release and there is the expectation of food. The situation is inherently stressful, and for nurture children, intolerable unless well managed. Waiting, choosing, managing trays and cutlery and relating to a wider group are all potential hazards for which they need preparation and support. Many teachers take their children into the dining hall and either stay with them or ensure that a familiar meals supervisor is there to help them. The difficulties are considerably eased when the teacher has lunch with them, particularly if they sit round a 'family' table. There is less trouble in the playground afterwards and most teachers feel that this extra time with the children is well spent.

The playground

Most schools now make strenuous efforts to make break times safer, more constructive and happier for the children by providing a range of activities from ball games to quiet areas. In some situations, excitement may reach a high level and provocation, unintentional or not, can be considerable. The sudden release of energy under unstructured conditions inevitably shows itself in aggressive behaviour, and the nurture children are not the only ones who cannot cope.

Nurture group children normally have breaktime with the other classes. The adults also need a break and the children need to feel part of the whole school; they must be seen by the other children to be part of the school and to be potential friends. Very out-of-touch children who cannot manage in situations of this kind are supervised inside but most go out. The timid, unventuring children are likely to attach themselves to the adults who are supervising, or they cling together. For the other children, there can be serious difficulties; they have insufficient personal resources and internalized structure and control to use the situation constructively, and cannot cooperate with others or tolerate anyone getting in their way. Dislike of physical contact is also common, and many of them see provocation where none is intended.

Preparation

The children need help in anticipating what might happen at playtime. A great deal of preparation is needed and this is repeated before playtime *every* day until controlled behaviour in the playground is an established pattern. The teacher describes the sequence of events from classroom to playground and the situations that are likely to arise there. Their feelings are anticipated in detail and they are told what to do. Instructions are repeated as often as necessary, attention is insisted on and procedures are rehearsed.

Playground supervision

It is important that the supervisor is known to the children. The nurture teacher goes to the playground with them and introduces them. They know they are to go to that person if there are difficulties. They also know where the nurture staff are, can go to them if they need to and are reassured to know that they really are where they said they would be.

If there are difficulties, the children concerned are brought back into school and the nurture staff re-assume responsibility for them. They sit quietly in the room and although not criticized are not given extra attention. Remaining in school during the break may be preferable to the playground and some schools provide quiet indoor activities as an alternative. The ultimate aim though is to help the children to learn to manage in the playground.

Playground organization

It is recognized that the playground is a difficult place for all children and that work has to be put into the physical surroundings, the facilities provided and the organization of the space. Structuring the time spent in the playground is also important and many schools shorten the lunchbreak to make it more manageable. School councils often have suggestions to make about improvements.

In some schools, all the teachers are in the playground just before the end of playtime, and the children line up by them when the signal is given. Lining up is usual where the level of disruptive behaviour is high.

Playground incidents

Inevitably, problems in the playground will arise, and it is the nurture child who is often at the centre of trouble. There are, however, two important stabilizing factors. They know where the adults are and that they can go to them if in difficulties, and this is a reassurance. They also know that the nurture staff will be told about incidents in the playground, and those involved will be taken to them or they will be brought out to deal with it. The situation may not be propitious. The supervisor may be upset and angry. Neither the child nor the supervisor is able to cope. It is clearly inappropriate to punish the child, though sanctions may be necessary and affirming of the fact that behaving properly in the playground is a requirement. It is not an option and has to be learned, although difficult. All that goes on in the nurture group contributes eventually to better behaviour in the playground, but specific attention to this is nevertheless needed and problems arising are not only anticipated and discussed beforehand but are talked through afterwards in the classroom.

Some children have no idea at all of what went wrong. Others can, with difficulty, be helped to think it through and put it into words. These are usually older children, and a great deal of time and patience are needed to obtain a reliable story. All the children concerned are in turn asked what happened, and what went wrong, and they have to sit and listen, and contain their outrage. Not surprisingly, an imperfect perception of the situation is common. Increased understanding usually comes only when the children have learned sufficient self-control to maintain some awareness of what is happening at the time, and the main value of talking through at this stage is to focus attention on the teacher's requirement for self-control, self-awareness and personal responsibility.

Playground games

In many schools, often where the level of tension is high, there is a relative absence of traditional, ritualized games. In addition, many of the children have no prior experience of learning to play with other children in a small-group situation that is less chaotic and confusing than that of the playground. Some are not allowed by their parents to play outside, watching television and videos instead or, more recently, have their lives 'programmed' with continuous adult-directed activities without opportunities for free play. Their talk suggests that they are receptive to undifferentiated themes, of which violence is the most striking. They accept this as normal behaviour, are imitative, and any games they develop in the playground are likely to have violent content. Structured play in the playground needs to include teaching children traditional and cooperative games as a whole-school activity. Active help from an adult in the playground, by providing ideas or direct leadership, is valuable, but most important is the attitude of all the adults in the school; they understand the children's difficulties, are alerted to what might go wrong, know how to deal with it and there is consistency of expectations and management.

The extended school day

Many of the children attend out-of-school clubs. This can be very difficult for them and nurture children who may be in the greatest need are often excluded (something that penalizes parents too and adds to the complexity of relationships). They cannot cope with the organized games offered, which, even when relatively simple, require many coordinated skills. The nurturing school recognizes the positive benefits of extended school provision and will ensure that nurture principles inform all school policies.

Celebrating festivals

Festivals are exciting times in schools. Staff will be sensitive to the festivals of the majority faiths and will want to help children to enjoy them. Preparations often start early and may build up to a climax of a concert or special assembly and perhaps a special meal. It is important to recognize that festivals can bring additional work and may be stressful for the adults who work hard to make them a success. They can also be an overwhelming experience for some of the children and may exacerbate their difficulties. The problems that arise are sometimes entirely unexpected.

In a KS2 school, when a film was shown in the school hall as a treat, the children ignored the screen and turned excitedly to the source of the light, nudging each other and exclaiming. The film was stopped and their attention was drawn to the screen. Then there was another unanticipated hazard. One of the characters when appearing for the first time was very amusing and they laughed. When he appeared again, he was not funny but they laughed uproariously, inappropriately and disruptively. The teacher was disappointed by their behaviour. The film was stopped again and they were taken back to class. The incident was talked through and the adults now understood what had happened; 'We'll try again', they said, and the children were able to follow the film at a second showing.

In another KS2 school, the children had been carefully prepared for a supervised and well-rehearsed musical parcel game. They all went to the Christmas party in the school hall and took part well, but in the parcel-passing game, one of the boys was unable to contain his excitement. He tore off the wrapping with his teeth when he should have passed the parcel on, and stuffed the chocolate bar into his mouth. This was a child who did not know when he came into the group that he had five fingers on each hand.

All that can be done in school when festivals approach is to slow the pace, control the excitement and regulate the extent of participation in the school activities in accordance with the coping capacity of each child. Nevertheless, in spite of the problems and stress, most children in the nurture groups are able to make a modest contribution to the school festivities, and respond with pleasure to the special happenings at this time. Success is possible when there is careful organization and a sympathetic attitude in the school as a whole.

Sometimes children leave a situation of heightened stimulation and high expectation in school, and go home to restricted conditions where nothing special is happening. There may be no presents and if they take home with pleasure a present for their parents made in school, it may not be well received. The gesture may intensify the parents' depression and sense of deprivation, and the feeling that they are failing their child as they feel themselves to have been failed by others. In some homes, the present may be an unwelcome intrusion. Far from being a festive occasion, for many families, it is a time when a sense of deprivation, loneliness and alienation is at its most intense. Tempers are likely to be frayed and recriminations rife and the exuberance of demanding children can be the last straw. Other families, equally under stress, are kept highly charged by a wild rush of noisy and overstimulating parties which keep everyone up all night long.

Many of the children are kept indoors during the holidays. For much of the day, there is little to occupy them and any presents provided may be unsuitable or readily broken, and cause frustration. For a long period of time, they are in an unusually stressful situation, and have usually lost ground when they return to school after a holiday.

School trips

Many children in nurture groups have an unusually confused and fragmented picture of the world beyond home and school. New arrivals to the UK may never have been on a bus, and when taken onto the top deck, think the bus is falling over, or dash from side to side, not connecting up the views but treating each as though a separate television screen. Some have never been in a shop and are frightened or overwhelmed by the experience, or intoxicated by the mysterious and exciting things they see.

Trips are part of the curriculum; they are introduced gradually and with careful preparation. Simple trips come first and must be manageable and any trip suitable for a family with pre-school children is likely to be successful. However simple, detailed planning is essential, and all the children are thoroughly prepared for a new experience, even if this is only a slight extension of something they have done before, and all possible deviations from the familiar pattern are anticipated. The teacher describes how excited they feel, verbalizes their likely fears and explains that if they feel excited or frightened, they must not rush about and disturb other people but must tell one of the adults about it instead. Not all problems can be foreseen.

> One assistant took four children to a supermarket. They were used to going to small local shops and at first all went well. Then one of the children spotted the contents of a burst packet of rubber bands, scattered on the floor. All the children swooped on the rubber bands and crawled on the floor to retrieve them. Chaos followed.

Usually, though, with good preparation, they are rewarding experiences. Another teacher and assistant took their children to the Science Museum, and the teacher later said with pride: 'There were lots of other classes there, but *we* were the best behaved of all.'

Shopping

It is usual for the children to go shopping with one of the adults and another TA, only one or two at first then gradually, with careful mixing, building up to bigger groups. Young children hold hands and quickly learn to behave well. The first visits are usually to the local shop to buy food for the group. They go regularly in turn and it becomes a routine event. Some of them pass the shop each day on their way to school and could go alone, but need and respond to the security and warmth and the very special pleasure of the shared enjoyment of an adventure. Some talk very loudly when they first go out, and have difficulty in walking in an orderly way, others are overwhelmed, whisper to the adult and cling tightly. For those who know about shops and have the anxiety of domestic responsibilities at home, it is an opportunity to learn to choose and to count out the money in a situation which is carefree and enjoyable. For all of them, it is a needed extension of experience and for many is an exciting adventure, and they ask questions and comment eagerly. They might also visit the bank, the launderette and the post office and later go to the supermarket with a breakfast or birthday shopping list. They carefully take items from the shelf and queue without jostling the others. Occasionally, they go to the cafeteria and enjoy learning the procedure, choosing what to have and behaving well.

Social visits

Many staff of the early groups lived locally, and if a visit to their home was suggested, the children anticipated this with eagerness, and it was immediately a favourite event. They had a drink and a biscuit there and behaved well. This would no longer be appropriate but the experience can be replicated by a visit to the nurture group in a nearby school that is within walking distance or a short bus ride away. The visiting children can take flowers or bake a cake.

> The children in the host school had prepared food and handed this round with pride, and enjoyed showing their guests how to play with their toys. Invitations and thank-you letters, written individually or by the teacher in collaboration with the class, were part of the experience and added to the pleasure and interest of the occasion, as well as having social and educational content.

The local park

The children's limited knowledge of their local environment can be salutary. The younger or more inhibited children are timid and overwhelmed, and cluster round the adults, frightened to leave them and uncertain of what to do. The older and more outgoing ones seem intoxicated by the experience. They strain as though on a lead and when 'released', rush round in circles at tremendous speed.

> The teacher of the first KS2 group described how one of them tended to lead and the others would run after him, then another would go off in a different direction and they would then all follow him. They seemed intoxicated: 'They didn't look but seemed to need to touch ... excited, but greedy. They see; they want.' They sulked and got into fights, squabbled, had tantrums and returned to school exhausted. This greedy quality was no longer apparent by the summer term, and in the park they fed the ducks, ran for the swings and played ball together.

Longer trips

The short, local trips are most important: two or three times a week to the shops and a half-day in the local park every two weeks or so. These regular excursions are opportunities for the children to experience and begin to notice small changes that happen in the familiar world around them. Later in the year, some of the groups are able to manage a whole day away. Outings in the country, or locally if there is plenty of space to run, are preferred and shopping for food and preparing a picnic lunch beforehand is an important part of the event. Often, they are more interested in what there is to do, see and collect rather than playing games. A visit to a farm is usually successful and towards the end of the year, when the children are more experienced and are accustomed to going out, visits to museums or the zoo with their mainstream class are manageable. These more formal trips are treated as special occasions; they require an adequate level of organization and experience but for some they have no relevance.

A great deal can be built into any of these trips. There is the shared anticipation, the experience itself and then sharing the experience. At first, few of them remember, or appear to experience anything other than the basic, dramatic or personally relevant things, like seeing two dogs in a fight or being stuck in a tunnel in the train. They need a lot of help in noticing and remembering at the time, and some may need to be told beforehand to try to remember one thing to tell the others when they get back to school. As they become more experienced and controlled, they notice and remember more. The adults elaborate and develop the situation in language, making personal links for the children that extend their experience, evoke imagery and give feeling to it. They help them to notice the warmth of the sun on their faces and the crunch of leaves beneath their feet, and although some of them say very little, they begin to take in a great deal, and gain a greater awareness of themselves and their feelings. Treats, on these trips, are a shared indulgence, an affirmation of the shared satisfaction of the experience, and the relationship that supports it. Trips are also an important contribution to class identity, and provide a bank of class memories of events and feelings that can be recorded in photographs, to be recalled at leisure. They lead to observations and comparisons, and evoke links with other events. They also enhance awareness and acknowledgement of the children for each other, and encourage conversation.

Managing behaviour on trips

The behaviour expected on a trip is solely to ensure each child's enjoyment and the well-being of the group as a whole. In spite of all the care that is taken, and the very reasonable restrictions imposed, not all trips go well. Planning must include a risk assessment and the management of any inappropriate behaviour. This may mean taking additional adults and ensuring the availability of a member of staff on call at school. The children remember occasions like this and sometimes refer to them: 'That was when I didn't go.' Children needing to be taken back to school get no special attention though care is taken to acknowledge them later.

Trips with their mainstream class

Nurture group children usually join their mainstream classes for trips. They seem to realize that certain expectations have to be met and sometimes ask afterwards: 'Were we good?' On occasions like this, the nurture practitioners find it helpful to give them special reminders to help them manage on their own. The children take pleasure in learning what to do on these outings, and in behaving well. This is an important step in consolidating their membership of the class and their growing sense of themselves as responsible and independent learners (see Chapter 10).

Summary ☐

- Cognitive development is intimately linked to the child's emotional and social development and cannot be separated.

- The nurture curriculum is inclusive – it contains crucial cognitive and emotional experiences for future learning.

- Practitioners know and exploit the learning content of everyday experiences – speech, language and communication are emphasized.

- The National Curriculum is taught at the level most appropriate for the child.

- It is essential that all school policies include reference to the nurture principles and cross-reference with the nurture group policy.

Further reading

DCSF (2008) *The EYFS Inclusion Development Programme (IDP): Supporting Children with Speech, Language and Communication Needs*. London: The Stationery Office. These inclusion materials are excellent resources for nurture practitioners.

Keenan, T. and Evans, S. (2009) *An Introduction to Child Development*. London: Sage Publications. See section 3 which explores further the aspects of developing autonomy identified in this chapter.

Maynard, T. (2007) 'Forest Schools in Great Britain: an initial exploration', *Contemporary Issues in Early Childhood* 8(4): 320–31.

O'Brien, L. (2009) 'Learning outdoors: the Forest School approach', *Education 3–13* 37(1): 45–60. The Forest School is a refreshing look at developing environmental studies and outdoor play, particularly for older children. Information can also be accessed at www. forestschools.com

Part 3

SETTING UP A
NURTURE GROUP

School and Community Cohesion

> The aim of the nurture group is the successful return of the children to their mainstream classes. This chapter sets the context for successful practice incorporating nurture group principles in schools at the beginning of the 21st century through:
>
> - a whole-school policy which is understood and supported by everyone in the school
> - a school staffing structure with clear responsibilities and accountability
> - a recognition of the relational aspects of school organization and the importance of working in partnership with others both within and beyond the school
> - positive attitudes and an ethos which facilitates personal and professional development.

Gaining informed support

The support of school governors for establishing a nurture group is essential; their role in school evaluation and school improvement will determine their subsequent involvement.

The nurture group is a Special Needs intervention at School/Early Years Action Plus of the SEN Code of Practice (DfES, 2001b). The SEN Coordinator (SENCO) is responsible for coordinating provision, liaising with class teachers and teaching assistants and through this will have a considerable influence on attitudes. Professional development should include office staff, supervisory assistants and governors, as a nurture group which works in isolation can exclude them from ownership or responsibility for the children. Staff with a query, doubt or concern need to be able to approach the nurture group staff directly; this prevents misunderstandings developing.

Referral to the group

As well as the practicalities of referral (see Chapter 10), the process provides opportunities for professional development and dialogue. School staff should be introduced to the thinking behind the procedures for referral to the group as well as to the referral forms and developmental assessments that will be used, particularly the Boxall Profile. The procedures and rationale for contacting and involving parents and carers need to be discussed and established. Nurture group staff work collaboratively with school staff in order to make valid referrals and to ensure a new child is introduced to the group with care and sensitivity. A new group should not be hurried; the nurture staff must have time to prepare the room and devise a manageable programme of initial assessment and ongoing record-keeping which will inform future curriculum planning for the group. The more potential difficulties are foreseen and planned for, the greater the chances of success.

The nurture group's professional profile

It is important that the intervention offered by a nurture group is seen as a vital part of the inclusive curriculum offered by a school. To this end, the involvement on a regular basis of the senior management team, SEN governor and class teachers will be beneficial in validating the work of the group. This might be achieved through:

• invitations to join the group for breakfast occasionally. These can be written and delivered by the children who will be delighted if their class teacher can join them in the group

- sharing good work
- a display board/area in the main body of the school where examples of the nurture group children's achievements can be on show
- a regular time for friends from their mainstream class to visit and join in (although not when a child is first admitted to the group)
- a regular slot at staff meetings/SMT for reporting back on work achieved and the progress of the group
- an annual report to governors
- application for the national quality Kitemark for nurture group practice when appropriate.

Expectations, outcomes and boundaries

The children taken into nurture groups are usually at least two to three years below their peers in all areas, especially in their social and emotional development. They need planned and organized experiences and a great deal of direct support. The nurture practitioners provide consistent boundaries and expectations and the children benefit from the establishment of rigorous routines and begin to understand cause and effect.

The mainstream classroom provides an experience that for a child is both complex and stimulating. The class teacher would have to be strict and repressive with children who are undeveloped and disorganized, but in the structured, more relevant context of the nurture group, they are able to engage with experiences through a more personalized structure. The controlled situation of the nurture group contains the children's anxiety and enables them to function and to achieve success.

Responsibilities and relationships

Positive relationships are helped by having systems and structures that are clear and understood by everyone; communication is facilitated so the day-to-day running of the school happens smoothly; and time and energy are used productively for the benefit of the children rather than spent dealing with problems and misunderstandings. The generic responsibilities for personnel involved with the nurture group are listed below and can be adapted to meet the needs of individual schools working within a particular local authority (LA).

The head teacher

The head teacher has overall responsibility for the functioning of the nurture group within the school. S/he is responsible for:

- the operational management of the nurture group, including the arrangements in the case of absence of the nurture group staff or closure of the nurture group
- management of the nurture group teacher as a member of the school staff
- management of the nurture group assistant as a member of school staff
- oversight of the curriculum planning and monitoring of work within the nurture group
- ensuring that the nurture group teacher participates in the school's agreed performance management procedures
- ensuring that health and safety procedures are followed in accordance with the school's policy
- ensuring that the nurture group operates within the guidelines of the LA's policy statement on equal opportunities and the school's SEN policy documents
- complying with any LA requirements regarding nurture groups.

The school SENCO

The SENCO is responsible for:

- other responsibilities as determined by individual schools
- liaising with the nurture group teacher and class teacher – this will include the development and implementation of Individual Education Plans (IEPs) if required
- being involved in reviews as required
- overseeing, monitoring and supporting the successful reintegration process.

The nurture group teacher

The nurture group is educational provision supported by the education psychology service. The qualities of a good class teacher with academic objectives are required and s/he must:

- be firm in setting limits
- have a clear knowledge and understanding of social and academic standards
- have the conviction to convey to the children that these expectations will be reached and maintained
- have the sensitivity and ease of rapport to relate constructively to other staff, governors and parents/carers
- ensure a close working relationship with the assistant in an equal partnership.

The nurture group teacher is responsible for the day-to-day management of the class. S/he has the following duties:

- carry out, and contribute to school policies and procedures, including child protection procedures where appropriate
- organize and plan the activities of the classroom, bearing in mind the individual needs of each child and drawing from the Early Years Foundation Stage curriculum
- be an advocate for and develop nurture group principles
- keep daily individual records of the children's progress and intended programmes of work
- coordinate the work of the nurture group assistant
- discuss the children's progress regularly with the educational psychologist and other professionals involved at School Action Plus
- work actively in partnership with parents/carers
- liaise with class teachers, collaborating in curriculum planning and attending regular reviews under the Code of Practice
- identify strategies to help children manage less structured times of the school day such as play- and lunchtimes
- participate in continuing professional development (CPD) and joint planning with the class teacher and school SENCO regarding IEPs.

The nurture group assistant

- The nurture group assistant is employed in the nurture group full-time, working under the direction of the nurture group teacher.
- Her/his role is to assist the teacher in whatever tasks are necessary and to participate in appropriate In-service Education and Training (INSET).

The educational psychologist

The role here is to:

- attend regular meetings with the head teacher and nurture group team
- offer regular consultations and be involved in the selection of children for admission into the nurture group, their reviews and reintegration programme
- contribute to alternative action plans where reintegration is not appropriate.

Accountability

Nurture groups are evaluated through Ofsted inspection as well as any LA procedures. There needs to be agreement among the senior management team about the process for collecting data and evidence for the School's Self Evaluation Form (SEF), who is involved in the process and what their responsibilities are. Monitoring and reviewing the nurture group provision is an essential part of this ongoing self-monitoring responsibility.

It is advisable that the school's educational psychologist and/or any nurture group liaison officer from the LA are involved in the appointments of nurture group staff.

The School Improvement Manager for inclusion may also have a role in reporting to and liaising with the appropriate LA officer. The future provision and sustainability of nurture groups may well depend on staff with responsibilities in relation to the nurture group being proactive in their contact with LAs.

Support for the nurture teacher and assistant

A support system for the nurture group staff is essential, as is ensuring a work–life balance (DfES, 2003b). Although the numbers in the group are small at any one time compared to a mainstream class, over the course of a school year the staff may well be responsible for a larger number as children are gradually reintegrated into their classes. Many former nurture group children continue to need some degree of contact with the nurture group as long as they remain in the school and sometimes even after they have left.

The day-to-day work too is very demanding; it is complex and constantly changing as the children progress. It also involves a wider network of adult relationships than a mainstream class with both parents and other professionals. A supportive school environment which values their work contributes to all-round psychological health but it is invaluable for the nurture teacher and assistant to meet regularly with others doing the same work.

Meetings foster friendship and shared enthusiasm, and make it easier for anxieties and difficulties to be aired and shared. There is the opportunity to discuss new ideas and approaches and sharing good practice builds up confidence and increases job satisfaction and is a valuable form of CPD. In areas where nurture groups are well established, there is provision and, in some cases, a requirement for nurture staff to attend regular sessions of professional development.

An area of need which is less recognized and still to be addressed is for some form of supervision. Group and human relations related issues are frequently raised during workshop sessions at conferences or on CPD courses and indicate the level of insight that nurture staff gain through the work.

The nurture group's contribution to school improvement

The close observation of children and the meticulous attention to detail along with the ongoing conversation about the children's achievement and progress in all areas of their development is a powerful model for school improvement.

There is evidence that when nurture group principles inform all areas of a school's organization and curriculum, a positive cycle of growth and development is set in motion, reflecting at school level the micro level of the nurture group (Ofsted, 1997).

Relationships beyond the school

Partnership with parents and carers

Every school will have a policy on partnership with parents and carers. There is a lot of helpful guidance to schools available but schools with nurture groups might need to have additional strategies in place for hard-to-reach parents as many, like their children, have their own need to be nurtured. The Lamb Inquiry (DCSF, 2009c) has made a number of recommendations regarding special educational needs and parental confidence. The subsequent evidence submitted (Lindsay and Peacey, 2009) strongly endorses the value of partnerships with parents.

A referral to the nurture group, as with any other special needs provision, should not come as a surprise but, ideally, has been part of an ongoing conversation concerning the child's needs and how these can be met. Establishing positive links with and supporting parents is an essential part of the nurturing approach and they should be consulted at all steps in the process. In addition to the regular, formal SEN review meetings, nurture group staff take frequent opportunities, wherever possible, to see parents informally. In primary schools, this is often at the beginning or end of the day.

Open afternoons or evenings are often held termly and younger siblings are welcomed with their parents. A few parents have spent part of the day or the entire day in the nurture group, and they often accompany the children on trips.

It is apparent from the nature and quality of the relationship with some of the parents, essentially one of nurturance and friendship, that they themselves are being helped, both directly by their contact with the group and indirectly by the progress of their children. Some have maintained contact with the group after their children return to the mainstream class, or even after leaving the school. One teacher put it to a parent: 'We are in it together.'

Another commented: 'Most of the parents don't understand what has gone wrong and what we are doing. Those who do understand mind deeply, and are grateful.'

Close involvement of some of the parents in school could increase the isolation of those children whose parents rarely come, particularly as they are often the ones in most need. Sometimes strenuous efforts have to be made to engage them and occasionally the head teacher has to act in a more formal capacity to ensure contact.

Inter-professional collaboration and professional development

Nurture group teachers may work with a range of other professionals, including physiotherapists, occupational therapists and speech and language teachers and therapists, either with specific children or for suggestions for activities that would be useful for the nurture group as a whole (see Chapter 7). Their more circumscribed but intensive work is very relevant to that of the nurture group because they too 'begin at the beginning', but along separate developmental strands that come together in nurture work.

It is useful to distinguish 'early developmental learning needs' and 'special educational needs' to demonstrate the relationship between the two; they are not separate. Both provide experiences at an early developmental level, the one general, the other more intensively specific. Wherever possible, an element of shared professional development is offered which includes something of both. Integrated concepts and practice lead to a better service for the child, and equip the teacher to meet a wide range of needs. The special contribution of nurture work to an integrated course is its stress on the intermeshing nature of the different developmental strands at the earliest level. The implication is that all special needs work should be in a nurture context. Where this happens, the nurture group curriculum is enhanced.

The rationale of the nurture group thus provides a useful conceptual basis for a wide range of in-school and off-site provision for children with special educational needs. It is fundamental to the learning process and generates practice that is of relevance to all children with special educational needs.

Positive attitudes and ethos: a rewarding experience

It is usual for a primary school nurture group quickly to become, and be described as, the 'heart and hub' of the school. A secondary group is usually part-time and the approach focuses on developing the nurture group principles and social skills through the curriculum. Whether primary or secondary, the group increasingly influences the school's way of working and approach to the children's difficulties. Understanding comes about slowly through day-by-day interchange about specific children with other staff. They gain some idea of the rationale of the work, the way the group functions and the nature of the progress of the children. They become more aware of themselves and others, and draw unreservedly on this experience. The process is cumulative, irrespective of any focused CPD.

Nurture practitioners have a mature and demanding role in relation to other teachers, the parents and other agencies. It requires considerable personal reorganization and learning as they conceptualize their work within a broader educational context. In responding to the children as whole people, they become more aware of their own needs and the roots of their own behaviour and many have commented on the greater self-knowledge and self-realization this brings, and the sense of well-being.

'I'm a whole person for the first time with the children and I feel terrific.'
'I'm giving my whole self to the children, not just the teacher bit.'
'Being the teacher gets in the way.'
'The best years of my teaching life.'
'It all sounds so complex, but it's easy, really. All you have to do is be yourself.'

'Being yourself' is not easy for everyone, but nurture work is a way into being oneself, and the process is circular and the gains are cumulative. Adults and children grow together and, although the work is demanding and the task a daunting one, it is at the same time an exhilarating and energizing adventure.

The difficulties, the stress, the hard work and the doubts and fears, are very much like those of parents with young children. As with parents, the best way of bearing these is to have the support of each other and the readily available friendship of others in the same situation.

Summary ▢

- A whole-school policy which everyone in the school understands and supports is essential for a successful nurture group.
- All staff involved with the nurture group should have clear roles and responsibilities and understand how they relate to one another and are accountable.
- Nurture group staff work in partnership with others, both within and beyond the school; their positive attitude contributes to an ethos which facilitates personal and professional development for everyone.

Further reading

Bottery, M. (2004) *The Challenge of Educational Leadership: Values in a Globalized Age*. London: Paul Chapman Publishing. This text argues for mutual trust in school organization.

Fineman, S. (ed.) (2000) *Emotion in Organizations*. London: Sage Publications.

Lewin, R. and Birute, R. (2000) *Weaving Complexity and Business: Engaging the Soul at Work*. New York: TEXERE LLC. Both this book and the one above recognize that adult relationships and emotions cannot be separated from organizational structures.

Parents as partners – see www.teachernet.gov.uk for a checklist of the essential elements for a school policy.

9

School Improvement: Planning for a Nurture Group

Preparations for a nurture group are an expression of the schools' and nurture practitioners' commitment to Every Child Matters and their understanding of the needs of vulnerable children in the light of developmental and attachment theories. This chapter considers the indicators for determining the kind and level of nurture provision that will be most effective for school improvement and the factors which need to be considered for an action plan. Key issues are:

- the appropriate model of nurture provision for the school
- priorities for action to be shared with other staff and governors
- use of space, choice of equipment and furnishings.

Primary schools new to nurture work are strongly advised to start with a full-time group and modify their practice later, when they are more experienced. Where children in need of nurture-type help are a minority in an otherwise well-functioning class, they are likely to need a full-time group and for longer, because a high level of achievement will be required of them if they are to be successfully returned to their mainstream class. This might not be feasible at secondary level although consideration must be given to providing as much group time as is possible within the constraints of the curriculum timetable.

The appropriate model

These variants (see Chapter 1) would all be considered authentic nurture groups:

- a classic nurture group running for nine sessions a week, allowing one session (half a school day) for liaison, CPD, meeting parents, etc
- a part-time group run in the mornings with support to the children in the afternoons in their mainstream class
- two half-time groups at different levels
- full time (0.9) with varying numbers of children attending part-time.

Whatever the pattern, *nurture*-level children need to be full time in the group. Others actively benefit from greater contact with the mainstream class, particularly those *who need nurturing*, some of whom could be supported in the mainstream class with extra help.

Part-time attendance is more usual for older children and at KS3, provision is largely determined by the school's statutory curriculum requirements.

Decisions are made in relation to the total school situation, the proportion of children with special needs and the nature of their difficulties and the funding available.

Full-time groups and support

These groups provide experiences at the earliest childhood (0–3) level, and are for fundamentally deprived *nurture* children whose overall development is markedly limited. They have not reached the minimal level of personal and social competence of the EYFS and time spent in their age-appropriate class is wasted and stressful for everyone.

A full-time place is also appropriate for a new school entrant 'at risk' and will greatly reduce the possibility of failure in the mainstream class. Where there is no special resource to help these children, the only alternative to exclusion, which is happening on an increasing scale (Jones et al., 2005), is one-to-one learning support, a very costly use of resources. These children need close and continuing attachment and support within a carefully monitored and protected day as described in Part 2. This total nurturing environment is essential if they are to catch up with their peers in the mainstream class.

Many schools with nurture groups provide integrated support throughout the school and this enables children who would otherwise be full-time in the nurture group to remain part-time in their mainstream class from the beginning. These children are able to function to some extent at an age-appropriate level but they need the extra support of a particularly close relationship with an adult, and more intimate experiences and satisfactions, affection and reassurance than is possible in a large mainstream class. For some children, part-time nurture provision in conjunction with a modified mainstream class may be enough; others will need to be full-time in the nurture group.

In schools where severe deprivation and disadvantage are widespread, the overall organization and orientation of the school inevitably changes and implementing nurture principles becomes everyone's direct concern. It is usual for a full-time nurture group to be retained, but with considerable interchange of children on the periphery. The other classes, including the nursery, structure their day towards nurture principles and make nurture-level learning experiences a more explicit provision. The difference between the nurture group and the other classes is then largely determined by size, the smaller nurture class providing a more intensive input of earlier-level experiences for the most profoundly deprived children.

Half-time groups

Half-time groups are appropriate for children who can manage to some extent in the mainstream class. It is then usual for the morning group to be for *nurture* children and the afternoon group for *children who need nurturing*. Some schools run a morning group for a full range of *nurture* children, and in the afternoon the nurture practitioners work in their mainstream classes, giving direct support to the children in greatest need. This can be adequate for *children who need nurturing* but is not satisfactory for nurture-level children and may be contra-indicated, and is not the most effective and efficient use of resources.

Part-time groups

Where problems of deprivation are general in the school, children in special need are in the nurture group for two or three sessions a week, together with other more competently functioning children, for the especially close relationships and domestic and play activities possible there. This method depends on the whole school being run on coordinated nurturing lines. It has not been documented sufficiently well because of the large numbers of children involved, but anecdotal impression suggests that some children are sufficiently well organized and secure to relate to different people in changing situations, and benefit from greater involvement with the mainstream class. Early-level structuring and ambience of the school as a whole may make this possible but on the available evidence, the total time spent in part-time provision is far greater than it would be in a full-time group.

Children whose difficulties centre largely on lack of trust and poor self-image, and who respond to reassurance and support, and sometimes verbalization of their feelings, usually make good progress in a part-time group.

The experience provided by part-time groups of these kinds is likely to be helpful for those children with better developed experience and personal control, and is preferable for others loosely described as 'troubled'. It cannot, however, provide the wealth of broadly based and integrated earliest level experiences that are essential for nurture-level children.

Advantages and disadvantages of the different models

The full-time group is essential for children who are without adequate basic foundations for the mainstream class, but all possible links are maintained and encouraged. The nurture group is then within a nurturing school and the child's eventual integration with his peer group does not present a problem.

Half-time or part-time groups have limitations but many issues that need consideration in a full-time group do not arise, thus:

• any absence of the nurture teacher and assistant is better tolerated, because the children already spend half the day in their mainstream class and are familiar with the teacher and children there

- a run of bad behaviour is sometimes broken by a change of teacher at midday
- there are more opportunities for the class teacher to reinforce behavioural expectations and management, and the children see these standards as a more universal requirement. They have the satisfaction of knowing that when they please one teacher, the other teacher will know. This, too, reinforces the desirable behaviour
- aggressive behaviour in the mainstream class may be less of a problem than before because they become self-conscious about the consequences. They know they can talk about their difficulties afterwards in the nurture group, and this helps to contain feelings
- they benefit from being with children whose play and behaviour are more advanced
- communication between the nurture teacher and class teacher is more easily maintained because both are fully in touch with the child's needs and curriculum planning is more easily coherent. Opportunities and management in the mainstream class are more likely to complement and supplement the work of the nurture group. It does, however, require of the class teacher careful control of the children's experiences and meticulous acknowledgement of their achievements
- a class teacher who is less experienced with this approach has more opportunity to gain a developmental perspective on the children's difficulties in ongoing discussion with the nurture teacher
- full integration of the children within the mainstream class later is more straightforward because they are familiar with their class and the expectations there and the class teacher knows what they can do. They can cope with the loss of the nurture group because they know it is there if they need it.

A half-time or part-time arrangement may actively strengthen and consolidate the work being done in the nurture group. It presupposes, however, that experiences and controls have been at least minimally internalized and the child has some capacity for self-regulation, and some ability to reflect, anticipate and share. There are several advantages in a half-time group for such children, provided their curriculum needs are also being adequately met. The children are greatly in need of domestic and play activities (nurture curriculum) but also need nurturing and National Curriculum level work. Much of it stems from the child's immediate experience and this logically and naturally falls to the nurture teacher. It is important that while the class teacher retains overall responsbility for the child's progress, much of the teaching is the responsibility of the nurture teacher. Cooperation in curriculum planning is essential. The considerations for the morning and afternoon groups are therefore different, particularly as the work of the nurture group and mainstream class tend to be more focused on core subjects in the mornings, but in both cases there is a need to maintain a balance between basic structured work and more general experiences.

Whatever the school's final decision is, sympathetic rapport and good communication between the staff are of critical importance if children are to be successful in the mainstream class; their progress is maximized if the approach to their difficulties throughout the school is consistent and informed by nurture principles.

Size and composition of the group

The size of the group is important. Practitioners forming a group for the first time, particularly if many of the candidates are described as 'aggressive and disruptive', may well feel anxious about a group of up to 10 or 12. This is generally thought to be a useful and viable number, though some of the early groups, both at KS1 and KS2, were successful with as many as 14 and 16. Contrary to what might be expected, groups smaller than 12 do not necessarily function better, and it is undesirable for them to be less than 10. Small numbers are less satisfactory as:

- there is less scope for contriving a 'balanced' group and for influencing the dynamics
- the children see, and are part of, a narrower range of interactions and so have fewer opportunities for personal and social learning
- aggressive behaviour in a small group is more disruptive than in a bigger group

- loosening the child's ties with the nurture group is more difficult.

The composition of the group is important. As a general guide, no more than two-thirds of the children should be 'aggressive and disruptive' when the group is being formed, and pressure for more than this is resisted, particularly as children whose functioning is very limited become assertive as they progress.

The 'uninvolved' children are usually less often referred, partly because the teacher feels they will be distressed by being with the more 'aggressive' children, but also because their needs are less readily identified, overlooked even. These children may well be those identified in secondary schools for additional support through the Gaining Ground initiative (DCSF, 2009d). Resistance to referring children like this is usually resolved as the class teachers become more aware of the nature of nurture work and see the dramatic change in some of the children. Such children occasionally attach themselves to the group of their own accord.

There are advantages in having a group with a range of needs. Those who are timid and unventuring seem relieved that control is firm and gain security from the clear guidelines, routine and orderliness. They benefit from being with children who more readily involve themselves and are more demanding and assertive. They become drawn into their play, at first in a following or passive role, but when they see that it is 'safe', they start to shadow their activities and then begin to interact. They gain the confidence to assert themselves and to test out the limits. With children like themselves, they say little or nothing: there is little or no interaction between them, and to make progress they need a great deal of the adult's time.

The 'aggressive' children also gain. They see the more productive interaction between the adults and the less forthcoming children, and the satisfactions that are part of this. They become aware of the kindness and caring, and begin to understand that the teacher's control is part of the caring, and begin to take over a caring and controlling role. Often, they adopt the teacher's kindly supportive attitude to the 'unforthcoming' children, and with others more like themselves assert the requirements and impose controls. Their experience with children unlike themselves helps them to be more aware of themselves and each other, and is part of the process of learning to care for each other.

Preparing an action plan

Once it is decided within the School Improvement Planning process to have a nurture group, and the model which is most appropriate when balancing children's needs and the resources available, an action plan is required. This is likely to be the first task for the designated staff in consultation with the Senior Leadership Team and features in the four-day certificate course, Understanding the Theory and Practice of Nurture Groups. The action plan will identify:

- priorities: identification of children; selection of room and equipment; timetable; curriculum planning
- timescales
- key staff
- funding
- resources needed
- outcomes.

Most nurture groups begin at the start of the new academic year, in September, so ideally this preliminary work is done in the preceding summer term and the immediate preparations for receiving children during the first two weeks of the autumn term. This gives a reasonable amount of time for the final preparations to the room, observation and assessment of identified children (see Chapter 10), meetings with parents and the educational psychologist, final selection and completion of Boxall Profiles and collection of information.

The suggestions below derive from practice over time; modifications of organization and equipment will be needed in different situations and as circumstances change within the same school. Whatever the differences and ages of the children and the personalities and talents of the adults, the full range of early childhood needs must be planned for.

The nurture group room

There is rarely much choice of accommodation and considerable ingenuity may be needed to devise a physical environment appropriate for a nurture group day.

The type of room

An enclosed area is essential because the children must feel secure and contained. With 10 to 12 children on roll, two adults and extra visitors from time to time, the room should be big enough for about 16 people. A traditional classroom of generous size is satisfactory; it can be made to feel containing, and yet is big enough for free movement and play, and a wide range of domestic and school activities.

The location of the room

The allocation of a room should ensure that the underlying principles can be met. Some secondary schools have space within their existing special needs departments or in some cases purpose-built spaces have been created within the Academies or Building Schools for the Future programmes.

A readily accessible room in a central position is preferred. This makes possible an easy flow of children and adults, in and out, and ensures that the group is seen to be fully part of the school. It is likely to become the pivot of the school when nurture needs are widespread and the group is used flexibly.

Most young primary school children quickly acquire a concept of the school as a whole, and the head teacher fits spatially and functionally into this pattern of events and relationships. The head teacher, for nurture children, is essentially an extension of the group, and is their main reference point. S/he will have a warm relationship with the children, be associated with well-being and security and ease the children's transition into mainstream school life. Her/his relationship with the nurture staff is close and supportive, and reinforces their authority. This gives the children the extra security of knowing that the person who looks after them is looked after by someone else, and is a model of the supportive/dependency nature of relationships.

The phase manager and SENCO will also become familiar and trusted figures and part of a wider world.

Easy access to outdoor classroom space is desirable, ideally specific to the nurture group, and toilets should be within easy reach.

Organizing and equipping the room

Nurture practitioners need to have a clear understanding of early developmental needs when organizing the room and buying equipment.

Early years educational equipment is often seen to be appropriate; for older children and *those who need nurturing*, this may be the case, but it is not so for nurture children who have missed out on the very earliest experiences. Like expectant parents, they are preparing and choosing for a vulnerable and totally dependent baby, and it is important that, whatever the age range of the prospective group, they take up this from-birth perspective. This draws them immediately into a highly motivated and personal interest in the behaviour and learning of young babies (Gopnik, 2009; Gopnik et al., 1999; Robinson, 2003) and the items which will engage their attention.

Health and safety

All equipment in the room and anything done to make it 'homely' must meet health and safety requirements. *Everything has to be completely stable and remain so, even when assaulted by a child in a tantrum. Anything with projecting metal is unsuitable.*

Creating a nurturing ambience

Most nurture group children have internalized very little coherent experience and have little or no sense of well-being and purpose; they need to feel relaxed and calm to fully absorb the earliest childhood satisfactions gained through close physical contact with the adults. The environment is both home and school for children. Practitioners have frequently been very imaginative and creative with an unpromising room.

The following details are a direct response to schools' queries and concerns. Reflecting on what appears mundane can give a valuable insight into how a child may perceive something that as adults we take for granted – for example, how often do we as adults look at the classroom from the child's eye level?

The windows

Most 'nurture' children give their attention only to the meaning-ful world within the walls of their classroom. Events beyond this are of only occasional and limited interest. For others, the window provides lively experiences which they share excitedly with the adults. Some are interested but need an adult to point things out, to comment and explain, and inject feeling and meaning as a par-ent would. These experiences are for the most part incidental, but it is nevertheless an advantage for a KS1 group to have an inter-esting view, and for the windows to be just low enough for the children to look out.

The size of the windows is important. An extensive area of glass does not provide needed visual boundaries and a sense of physical containment, so it is helpful to partially obscure a big window with curtains. If the window is from floor to ceiling, and other children playing outside can look in, a painted scene could cover the lower panes. Some nurture group children overreact to adverse physical conditions, others under-respond or appear not to notice at all, so the adults are particularly alert to conditions likely to cause irritability and tension. Blinds or net curtains may be needed for the window and curtains for the home area.

Lighting and electric sockets

Lighting is important, again especially in the home area. Ideally, lights in the nurture room are at a lower level than a normal class-room but must be secure. In a new build, or if re-wiring is possible, wall lights above the children's reach are good. All lights should be shaded, to give a softer light. Some children see only naked bulbs at home.

Electric sockets are needed in the kitchen area and for a computer in the work area.

The arrangement of the room

Most nurture classrooms have four areas of roughly equal size: a home area, a kitchen area, a work area and a play area. It is usual for the work area to be nearest the door, so that the first impression is of an ordinary classroom. The home area is in the corner of the room that can be made the most inviting and comfortable, and is often by the window.

The home area usually connects with the play area on one side and the kitchen area on the other. These areas are flexible, and with judicious arrangement of the furniture, the space given over to each at any one time can be varied. Thus, a sofa can be extra seating in the home area and can be used during play as well as providing the comfort of a bed. Clearly defined areas and functions are important when the group is newly formed and always when the children are poorly organized.

The home area

Ideally, the entrance to the home area is wide with enclosing furniture low enough for an adult to look over. It is the focal point of the room; the children play there a great deal and some are there virtually all the time at first. *The home area is not the 'home role-play' area. It is the comfortable carpeted area where the children are collected together many times during the day for hand games, stories and chat.*

Mobiles

Classroom ceilings are often high but the apparent height of the ceiling in the home area can be reduced by stringing mobiles across the room, most conveniently across the home and play areas together. Anything the children have made is put up: aeroplanes, animals, faces, etc., along with shapes that are colourful or shiny.

Wallpaper

The home corner is usually papered up to domestic ceiling height and wallpaper covers the backs of outward-facing cupboards, giving a feeling of wholeness and containment. Warm colours are popular and subdued colours and patterns are less stimulating and distracting.

Furniture

Inward-facing cupboards with shelves above are needed to display storybooks, ornaments, photographs, games, toys and things made or cherished by the children, and have storage space below for toys and equipment. The home area usually has a big sofa, and sometimes two or three armchairs, all with padded arms.

A sofa in the home area provides valuable seating space and with blankets is a place to snuggle into. Car rugs are multipurpose and can be used for tents. In one school, the children broke the doll's pram because they climbed in it themselves, so a large shallow padded basket that was big enough for a child to curl up in became an important item. For both KS1 and 2 groups, there should also be a large container, such as a cardboard packing box which can be reinforced and have cushions to serve as a cradle, though more often it becomes a boat or a hideaway. A patchwork rug made of materials of different textures, colours and patterns is valued and children like to lie on it, stroke and cuddle it, and it is useful for lining a box to make a cot or snug hideaway. A low coffee table in KS2 or 3 groups is a focus for talking around at breaktime. It is rarely possible to have a dining table in the room, but school work tables covered with a tablecloth are satisfactory for a 'family' meal and it is usual for this to be in the work area.

Soft furnishings

Cushions are important. They make the home area welcoming and interesting, add to the comfort and are useful for imaginative play and for the release of feelings. Those with appliquéd animal faces or in the shape of animals are popular, particularly for older children who may not immediately take to soft toys. Some of the children are frightened of animals and are scared to touch fur, so animal cushions, incorporating fur, help them to get used to animals. Two-sided cushions, one side having a smiling face and the other a sad face, can be made in school with the children helping with the cutting and sorting. This is a purposeful, enjoyable activity with the adults and mathematical language can be introduced. Older children with help have made personal cushions with their names embroidered on. Texture, contrast, pattern and colour are important when choosing the coverings. Large bean bags or floor cushions are useful as the children like to lie on them on the floor, and sit on them during storytime.

A mirror and a clock

A full-length mirror screwed onto the wall is essential here or in the play area. A shop-style mirror is ideal. In one school, the staff felt that the area near the door should be welcoming and so furnished this as the home area. A full-length mirror was installed just inside the door, which was left open, and they found that other children in the school regularly stepped inside to look at themselves. A clock with plain, well-defined numbers is needed, and is best in the home or work area.

Photographs

As soon as possible, photographs of the children are displayed, preferably enlarged and framed, and they should have at least one photograph of themselves to take home, if they want to. Photograph albums of class activities and outings are usually kept in the home area. These are important for recalling and describing happy occasions in the group and sequences of events, and in gaining a sense of time. They also contribute to group and personal identity. It is usual to have plants or flowers here and the more personal things the children have made in school.

Soft toys and dolls

How these are used is described in Chapter 6.

A wide range of soft toys is needed and are equally important for older children. Animals are popular, particularly teddy bears.

Clowns with a happy face on one side and a sad face on the other, or happy/sad, asleep/awake, upside-down dolls are useful. It is important to have at least one that is roughly child-sized, that is soft and yielding but firm enough to sit on a chair and not too awkward to carry. They are incorporated into play and work sessions and are important members of the group and are spontaneously used to express feelings, and for the enactment of anxieties and problems. Current cult figures, too, are popular.

A well-equipped group has dolls of many different kinds and sizes and of different racial types. Rag dolls made in school are particularly enjoyed because the children know they have been made especially for them. In addition, every group has at least one commercially produced doll for the children to bath, preferably one that will not easily get smashed in a tantrum. Clothes for the dolls are usually made in school and the children watch with enjoyment and interest. They are made in great variety to provide scope for changing the dolls and for gaining concepts of size, shape, area and one-to-one correspondence.

Cradle and pram play

The home area in primary groups needs opportunities for cradle and pram play. There are objects to suck, chew and shake; squeaky toys and rattles, soft balls and small textured soft toys; and over the sofa a mobile that swings and makes a noise, for example plastic cartons glued together with beans inside. Spinning tops, wobbly clowns, nesting, stacking, posting and pull-along toys, and a hand-held baby mirror and the Discovery or Treasure Basket are conveniently kept in the home area because the children usually play with them there.

For those children who need to suck and chew, the teacher provides suitable personal things, as hygiene has to be considered.

The kitchen area

The kitchen area usually takes up to one-quarter of the total floor area and is useful as an overspill for academic work or for play.

Facilities may be no more than a classroom sink and a socket for an electric kettle and toaster but every effort should be made to set up a recognizable kitchen area. Opinion concerning the height of tables and fitments is towards the lowest domestic height available. This is awkward for some of the children but the experiences they need are those normally gained in the kitchen at home.

Equipment

A cooker is standard equipment and should be of domestic size, with four hobs and an oven and must meet safety regulations. Schools which have a fully equipped kitchen area have preferred a kitchen sink with a double drainer; the children can then stack, wash and dry. Cupboards are needed for food storage. Other equipment includes cups, saucers, mugs, plates, preferably in an unbreakable material, knives, forks and spoons; whatever cooking and baking equipment is available, if possible including balance weighing scales, a kitchen timer, measuring beakers and a funnel, and domestic pans. All these items also lend themselves to work with mathematical concepts. If a refrigerator is available, the racks should be fixed in place for safety.

Cleaning equipment is needed, if only a brush and a dustpan, as clearing up sometimes involves simple cleaning and is done as though with a parent. An ironing facility is useful if safety considerations permit. Dolls' clothes and cushion covers and sometimes children's clothes need to be washed and ironed from time to time.

Cupboards and drawers

Visual prompts of the contents of the cupboards, and recipes displayed on the cupboard doors, introduce symbolic representation and are useful for language work. It is convenient to have somewhere to keep tablecloths or place mats, tea towels, hand towels and aprons and hooks for those in use. The children take it in turns to set the table so there should be a drawer for class cutlery, one that is easy to pull out and carry around, or a cutlery tray.

Food preparation

Simple food can be prepared even with very limited equipment and essential personal and social learning experiences are built in. A well-resourced kitchen area provides a wealth of opportunity for practical activities. The learning outcomes are considerable: the pleasurable atmosphere and shared experience reinforce attachment; visuo-motor-spatial skills, language and logical sequencing of activities are inherent in the process; and mathematical and scientific concepts can be developed. The budget and space dictate what is possible, but groups in cramped surroundings have managed happily with an electric kettle and a toaster, or even nothing closer than the facilities of a distant staff room, used only for cooking.

The play area

This is usually at least one-quarter of the room, but the space available for play is effectively far bigger because a lot of quiet play takes place in the home area, and often the only place for wet and messy activities is the kitchen area. The clean and dry play area is usually carpeted or has a vinyl-type floor covering. In a primary school, it is stocked with nursery and infant equipment, and has a furnished role-play area, an adaptable frame for use as a shop, large building bricks, pull-along toys, dolls, telephones, etc. Large pieces of material of different size, shape, pattern and texture provide intense pleasure from feeling, burrowing into and swirling in them, draping and dressing up, and the adults, as appropriate, introduce basic language and mathematical concepts. It is important to have a baby-buggy or preferably an old pram that is strong enough for a child to sit in and be pushed around in.

Sand and water are important and the equipment includes bath toys as well as funnels, sieves, etc. Most groups have a table for clay and paints. These materials are used under strictly defined conditions, and in some cases under supervision, as some children need help in using them constructively, while others need to mess and slosh.

A large sand tray, preferably with a lid, is best placed in a corner so that only two children can use it at a time, and should have gravel and pebbles as well as sand. Ideally, the water tray should be like the sand tray, but with tap and drain, and fixed in the corner at kneeling height. A large, plastic washing-up bowl is useful for water play for one child. These are covered when not in use.

The work area

This is roughly one-quarter of the floor space. Two tables, each of one metre square, and two tables, one metre by one-half metre, make a satisfactory and flexible combination. Furniture size is according to need rather than age. Otherwise, there should be cupboards with shelves, provision for storage of books, work trays, a paper store unit, a small movable whiteboard, a display board and a computer. A one-hour kitchen timer is useful for timing work, and as an incentive for persistence and controlled behaviour.

The computer

Few children in the group have the higher-order competencies required for the computer. They need to develop fine visuo-motor skills, and to see visually evident cause and effect in the real world, and to have a notion of symbolic representation before they are ready for this. It has a function for children who have consolidated this earlier stage and need an introduction to the computer skills required in their mainstream classes, and for children who have emotional and social needs at an early level but are cognitively better organized and competent and are able to work at their National Curriculum level. Care must be taken, however, to ensure that it does not become a barrier to social learning; particularly at KS2 and 3, the solitary nature of the activity might easily become an avoidance of cooperative and collaborative play and work.

Materials, toys, games and equipment

Nurture groups cater for the classic nurture child who may be at the 18-month level or less, and also for children who have emotional needs but are cognitively more competent. The equipment needed in any group is likely to vary from year to year but opportunities for the earliest childhood experiences are always available. Pets are unlikely to be appropriate at first and are introduced only later, with preparation, when the group is established and the teacher feels that the children have developed a sense of caring. They can then become very important in the group, especially for older KS2 and 3 children.

Opportunities for the release of energy are needed, such as a run in the playground and outdoor classroom and play equipment where there is space.

The appearance of the room

The overall appearance of the room is influenced by the method of intake, the stage the group as a whole has reached and the dominant needs of the children within it, but a comfortable relaxed home atmosphere is important. The equipment available covers the full range, but what is provided at any one time is determined by the needs of the children and teaching style.

At one extreme, in a school with widespread needs and many profoundly deprived children, all the toys except those in immediate use were kept hidden from sight in cupboards. Stimulation was reduced to a minimum because the nurture group was intended to be basic and short term for children coming from the nursery or new entrants felt to be at risk. From there, they moved on quickly to the mainstream class which was run on nurturing lines but with greater choice and more creative activities available.

At the other extreme, in a school with similarly widespread and severe needs, the group was in a double-size classroom with an unusually rich variety of early-level toys and equipment on view. These were arranged in colour-coded areas according to their intrinsic value and interest for the child: touch, sound, water play, etc. In this school, as in most others, the children remained in the nurture group until they could manage in a relatively unmodified mainstream class, and so the experiences available for the children who could use them were extended to KS1 activities.

Summary ☐

- Schools which have identified nurture group provision within their School Improvement Plans in order to meet their responsibilities under Every Child Matters will ensure that the practical preparations they undertake reflect their understanding of and commitment to the underlying principles and theories.

- The preparations needed are formulated in an action plan which is shared with all staff.

- Decisions concerning the use of space, choice of equipment and furnishings are guided by the practitioners' perception of the earliest developmental level and needs of the children rather than conventional school resources.

Further reading

Bishop, S. (2008) *Running a Nurture Group*. London: Paul Chapman Publishing. This book contains a lot of practical advice.

Gopnik, A. (2009) *The Philosophical Baby: What Children's Minds Tell Us about Truth, Love and the Meaning of Life*. London: Bodley Head.

Gopnik, A., Metzoff, A.N. and Kuhl, P.K. (1999) *How Babies Think*. London: Weidenfeld and Nicholson. Making decisions which are open to scrutiny by others can sometimes be intimidating, especially in a small school community. Both these texts are enjoyable, underlining the importance of making early-level provision for children who have missed out.

10

Assessment, Record-keeping and Evaluation

> The planning cycle in nurture groups begins with assessment. Reflective observation and effective assessment procedures enable practitioners to plan the best possible intervention. This chapter describes the rationale and procedures which enable nurture group staff to:
>
> - select children and young people for the nurture group
> - admit them to the nurture group and record and monitor their progress
> - facilitate their return to the mainstream class
> - evaluate the work of the nurture group.

Selection: general considerations

School-based provision for children vulnerable to social, emotional and behavioural difficulties (SEBD) should reflect a continuum of need, from the insecure and poorly sustained child who is responsive to reassurance and support to those who are functioning so inappropriately that they cannot make progress in the mainstream class. Different forms of provision have been developed to meet these different needs (Frederickson and Cline, 2002), and however they are conceptualized, they usually involve a closer relationship with the child, and more personalized learning experiences than are possible in the mainstream class. To this extent, they have elements of 'nurture' although the rationale of the work is different.

The basic criteria for a place in the nurture group are:

• a need for experiences normally gained in earliest childhood (at the 0–3 developmental level) or, for older children and young people, at least two to three years before their chronological age
• the potential to 'catch up'.

These criteria may not be very different from other forms of intervention such as 'place2be' (Batmanghelidjh, 2006) which provides therapeutic and emotional support to children in schools. Where nurture groups differ is in the emphasis on the curriculum: nurture groups are an educational intervention and are about children's learning.

The expectation of the nurture group

The expectation of the nurture group is that children will make sufficiently good progress there within four terms, and become established in a mainstream class before leaving their present school and subsequently will continue to prosper.

Children for whom the nurture group is recommended

Nurture groups were originally designed for young children whose social, emotional and cognitive needs were at the 0–3 developmental level; their development in different ways has not progressed in a constructive organized way, sometimes from birth. Older children, who are at least two to three years below their normal age group in their social, emotional and cognitive development, have also been found to benefit when the principles are used to modify the curriculum and approach to their learning.

Nurture children

This part expands on the section in Chapter 1. The descriptions derive from teachers' observations and the children concerned were the source for the Boxall Profile (Bennathan and Boxall, 1998). From the beginning of nurture groups, reflective observation and assessment have been fundamental.

- *They do not engage appropriately with adults.* Some function barely at all and make no acknowledgement of the adult, or they pay attention and appear to be biddable but respond mechanically. Others are indiscriminate in their search for affection, or form dependent or immature relationships. Others, again, disregard the teacher and may be overtly resistive and negative. Eye contact typically is not normal: the children look past, through, stare fixedly or their eyes dart everywhere, giving attention to nothing. Lack of trust is usual; they do not relate to adults and will resist making a relationship. Others are immature in their approach and response.
- *They have limited resources and lack basic competencies.* They have limited resources for play and do not explore constructively. Their language and concept development, gross and fine motor skills are often poor. Their attention is difficult to gain and sustain, and they do not involve themselves constructively and with persistence in class activities, or engage with the events of school. In the inappropriate situation of the mainstream class, they show emotional and behavioural difficulties that are often severe and which sometimes seem bizarre.
- *They have limited social skills and poor peer group relationships.* Many are not able to wait and share, their tolerance for frustration is poor and some have temper tantrums. Communication and relationships with other children are usually limited and unconstructive. Some are aggressive and are involved in fights, and may be resistive, destructive, explosive and violent, and in some cases deliberately antisocial.
- *They are depressed in their functioning or distressed in more overt ways.* Within this picture of general underdevelopment are children who are untrusting and insecure, lack confidence and have low self-esteem. Some are overtly distressed and may be self-destructive in different ways, or show disconnected fragments of obsessional behaviour.

The potential to 'catch up'

The children's limited competencies are understood to be a reflection of their poor learning opportunities in the past. This is mainly due to limited or impaired attachment experiences at the baby stage, inadequate play and communication with the parent/carer in later infancy and restricted or impaired opportunity to give purposeful attention and to investigate, explore and play. Intrusive negative experiences that disturb or distort the learning process are quite common, and in some cases early development has been disturbed or disrupted by sudden loss, bereavement, other trauma or crisis.

Associated or causally related perceptual-motor difficulties are more prevalent than in the general school population, particularly poor gross motor coordination. In the younger children, there is also a higher than expected incidence of intrinsic, medically based difficulties, some directly relevant to formal learning in school, such as speech impairment and/or an intrinsic language delay, and others such as epilepsy less directly so.

The decision to admit the child into the group rests with the school in discussion with the parents. A psychologist's individual assessment is not usually necessary and is not a statutory requirement.

Intrinsic learning difficulties and disadvantage

Children from well-nurturing homes who have minor specific difficulties, sometimes multiple, in the context of overall limited functioning may also be considered for the nurture group. Speech and motor coordination are the most common and, particularly for children from disadvantaged homes, there may be a considerable learning difficulty. Their opportunities to experience and explore have been restricted, either independently of a medical, physical or language difficulty or because of it, and this leads to stress and an inability to cope in the mainstream class, which in turn leads to secondary emotional and behavioural difficulties. The overall picture they present is sometimes very similar to the more classic *nurture* child, particularly those with associated educational needs of a more specific kind. Although psychosocial stress may be no more than a subsidiary factor, the early developmental nature of nurture work and the curriculum meets their special educational needs and this is the criterion for their selection. Most of these children make considerable progress in the nurture group and integrate successfully in the mainstream class.

More extreme specific needs cannot be met in the nurture group, although a great deal of extra care and help can be given and reassuring progress made. A psychological assessment of cognitive functioning at the early referral stage cannot give a firm prediction and may be misleading. A more reliable guide is the children's progress in the nurture group. Here, they are likely to be more relaxed and secure and better able to engage. They communicate more, are happier and their emotional and behavioural difficulties are less evident. However, if they continue to have general learning difficulties in spite of more relevant help and opportunities, they are unlikely to transfer successfully to a mainstream class and commonly reach a plateau after one or two terms. When this stage is reached, it is important that they are seen by the educational psychologist for an individual assessment, as it becomes increasingly difficult for parents to accept that other provision is more appropriate. The decision to take a child like this into the nurture group clearly will be influenced by the nature of the difficulties of the other children.

Difficult diagnostic problems

Particularly difficult and controversial 'diagnostic' problems are presented by the small number of children whose emotional/behavioural and formal learning difficulties are attributed to ADHD (Attention Deficit Hyperactive Disorder). They are distractible, hyperactive, have a low tolerance for frustration, lack persistence and make very little progress. Some impulse-dominated *nurture children* may seem very similar, and the underlying nature of their difficulties is not always apparent until they have been in the group for some time, and even then there may be doubt. Overall, *nurture children* show greater variability in their behaviour and are likely to have periods when they are more settled and calm, particularly in an individual relationship with the adult. If their distractibility remains at a high level, they are referred for a medical and psychological opinion.

A rapidly increasing number of children's difficulties in forming relationships and engaging with learning are being attributed to ASD (Autistic Spectrum Disorder). These children often make good progress in nurture groups although they too may need further assessment and intervention if improvement is not sustained.

Children with multiple and complex intermeshing difficulties are extremely difficult to assess, but the nurture group or nurture-type provision is an ideal situation from which to do this. The clearly defined structure supports them, and management of the group and of individual children is appropriate, as are the experiences which are available. The adults' response helps to establish an attachment, a more constructive and confident attitude and better functioning.

Cultural discontinuity

Since nurture groups began, the cultural map has changed significantly. In many places, the earlier generation of immigrant families is now well integrated and is fully part of the local community, although different socio-economic related problems now exist, especially violent knife and gun crime. In other areas though, some families continue to live in difficult and disadvantaged circumstances, are estranged from the mainstream culture and are isolated within their own cultural group. They may insulate themselves from their surroundings in bewilderment and fear, and lead unusually stressed, depressed and restricted lives. Usually, these children are well cared for within the resources of their parents and are secure within their homes, but have a very restricted life experience and are not able to bridge the emotional, cultural and environmental gap between home and school. Typically, they are unventuring and withdrawn, or frightened and bewildered in the mainstream classroom, and sometimes disorganized and resistive; some seem 'frozen' and function like automata. They participate minimally and without constructive purpose in the life of the class. Most of them are not *nurture children* in the strict sense and schools familiar with these difficulties can usually provide sufficient help. Where the difficulties are extreme, the children are usually well placed in the nurture group. They respond to the comfort and affection, accept physical contact and 'attach'; they are reassured by the clear expectations and manageable experiences and their progress is often dramatic, particularly when the school is a source of support for the parents.

Refugee children have suffered a traumatic severance from their community and cultural roots, and sometimes from their families. They come into the strange environment of the UK school from a barely viable, usually temporary home base and rarely speak English. They, too, benefit from the nurture group.

In cases where English is the child's additional language (EAL) and is the central difficulty, broadly based EAL help is more appropriate. Where the central difficulty is not disadvantage and seclusion, but firmly held parental attitudes and beliefs that are at variance with the ethos of the school, the nurture group may be counterproductive and is likely to be rejected. Help based in the mainstream class or in a learning support group may be preferable.

Small-group 'nurturing' support: nurture group or an appropriate alternative

Other children appropriately placed in the nurture group have better developed skills and concepts, and their level of organized experience may be adequate for supported work in the mainstream class. In some cases, their organized experience is on a very narrow base and is sufficient for participation in formal activities but not for personal and social growth. Such children, for different reasons, are only loosely attached in homes that otherwise provide adequate nurturing care and basic opportunities for cognitive development. They do not usually cause concern in the nursery because they have sufficient competence to engage with activities of their choice. Their difficulties become more apparent in later Key Stages when the demands are greater and sustained on-task attention is required. The emotional and behavioural difficulties of these children are not primarily related to social stress and a general impairment of early nurturing care, and in this respect they are not typical nurture group children. They are not usually considered suitable for psychotherapy either. Their main need is for an educational environment where the tempo is slower than in the mainstream class, the pressure of events can be relieved, and their personal 'space' is protected. Trust, security and attachment can be gently established and relationships more delicately attuned. They feel a sense of comfort and well-being, re-assurance and approval, get pleasure from the relationships and activities, and have an outlet for both self-development and the expression of their difficulties in creative activities. Although some could manage with individual support in the mainstream class, it is rarely possible and is not cost-effective to provide there the breadth of organized personal and social experiences they need.

Children who need nurturing

These children fall into five broad groups:

- *Children from families under long-term stress.* There may be no seriously limiting or distorting environmental factors, but for different reasons there is clearly defined long-term stress within the home, for example chronic illness in a parent, including severe depression, or a disabled sibling. Such circumstances generate anxiety and stress in the whole family and limit the attention available to the others, who lose experiences they would otherwise have with and through the parents. They blossom in the nurture group.
- *Children who have experienced, or are experiencing, trauma.* The loss of a key relationship, through a traumatic event, will inhibit the child from engaging in the experiences and events of the mainstream class. They may be unresponsive, lack interest and initiative, seem traumatized, have impaired capacity to play and show marked symptoms of anxiety and sometimes obsessional behaviour. Some show more overt distress and, in some cases, anger. Such children have experienced the desolation of the loss of a primary attachment relationship, and with this a profound disturbance of personal identity.
- *Bereaved children.* Children might experience family mourning as a withdrawal of interest and affection, and feel a sense of responsibility and blame. Particularly when the loss has been of a sibling, the surviving child might experience a damaging intensity of protective attachment from the grieving parents, and some might identify with the dead family member to a pathological extent.

   The nurture group or other appropriate school-based support

resource can be a healing experience that helps them connect with their roots and function again.

Children like this are usually discussed with the educational psychologist. If the nurture group is indicated, careful thought is given to the nature of the difficulties of the other children in the group and the overall stability and level of control, and a contra-indication is a high proportion of older, 'aggressive' children.

- Some children are well cared for physically and their opportunities at home are often of a high order, but their parents are involved in time- and interest-consuming work. When the substitute or supplementary care they arrange is unsatisfactory and the transition negotiated too quickly and without adequate preparation, the children suddenly lose familiar support and direction, are confused and often resentful and angry. They respond well to the concern and support of the nurture group, or other similar resource on a part-time basis.
- Occasionally, parents reluctantly accept the nurture group on a part-time basis having refused psychotherapy. The group provides a sanctuary for these children, and an opportunity for them to express their feelings.

All these children could be equally helped in an alternative form of therapeutic group providing opportunities at a later developmental level. They are termed 'children who need nurturing', though in other contexts would have a different though equally non-specific designation. This distinction between *nurture* needs and *nurturing* needs is largely based on cognitive competence because the nurture group is an educational resource in an educational setting. A group where *all* children have nurturing needs and the content of the nurture group day is more advanced is *not* a nurture group.

Children for whom the nurture group would *not* be recommended

This includes:

- children with a long term need. The nurture group may be appropriate in concept but it is too short term

- children who need more intensive and circumscribed help
- better developed children whose early experiences and relation-ships are 'knotted up'. These may be more appropriately helped by psychotherapy, and a helpful first step would be discussion with the educational psychologist
- situations where the nurture group is contraindicated in rela-tion to all other available forms of provision that might be appropriate
- children who are likely to need special provision throughout their school years. They may be placed in the nurture group only exceptionally, as a planned intermediate stage.

When a place is offered for a 'doubtful' case, it is usually for posi-tive and clearly formulated reasons. Sometimes it is because referral elsewhere is not acceptable to the family, or the nature of the problem is not understood and further and continuing assess-ment is needed, or because no clearly better alternative is available. Occasionally, it is for goodwill within the school. Although the reasons are not very positive in these cases, the deci-sion is purposeful and, within the total context, is a relevant one.

Ensuring a viable group

Not all the children referred are appropriately placed in the group at the same time. If the group does not gel, it is likely to get an unsuccessful image and the children's sense of failure and rejec-tion will be increased.

When discussing referrals, both the basic principles underlying the selection of individual children and the ultimate composition of the group must be kept in mind. The nurture teacher will use the discussion to convey the rationale behind the work and what can be achieved. Conviction about the approach and an intellec-tual grasp of the concepts underpinning it are essential.

Input from the educational psychologist may be helpful initially to provide a broader context for the work of the group and an ini-tial screening. The nurture teacher will also involve class teachers in the more detailed structured observations and analysis of the Boxall Profile. Although relevant information should already be on record, the referral process is a useful administrative hurdle because it helps teachers be aware of the children's total situation, their strengths and difficulties within a broader perspective.

Integrated whole-school strategies

Some children are appropriately helped within the school generally:

- These children are part of an estranged and self-defined subculture and present considerable problems for the school. Their families have a lifestyle that is often well organized and loyal within itself but is delinquent to varying extents. They are not part of the mainstream of society, and although living physically within it, they disregard its expectations and norms. Their young are well established within their own culture and are brought up to adopt its attitudes. They are often well organized and competent within their own exclusive group but neither engage actively in school, nor relate positively to the teacher or even to the other children. Many are challenging and confrontational.
- Other children presenting somewhat similar but less serious difficulties for the schools are from families in adversity and estranged. They lack trust, expect nothing from others and give nothing, and are vigilant in protecting their own interests. They are tough survivors who treat school with suspicion and are challenging and self-asserting.

The nurture group is rarely appropriate for these children, may be counterproductive and is likely to be rejected by the parents. Whole-school strategies directed to helping the children to be more constructively involved in school are preferred.

- A small but increasing group of children dominate and manipulate their parents and expect to do the same with the teachers in school. They seem unaware or unconcerned about the effects of their actions on others but understand the mechanics of social interaction sufficiently well to control and dominate. They try to get what they want regardless of others. They make conditions, and deliberate defiance is not uncommon. Some parents collude with this and are resentful when their children are disciplined. The children need a clear and consistent demonstration of acceptable behaviour in the context of the mainstream class.

- Other parents, who are concerned and caring and have the personal and material resources to provide adequately for their children, are indulgent and compliant or restrictive, or differ in their management to an extent which leads to difficulties for the children, particularly at school. The nurture group is not usually appropriate though the parents may ask for this and are reassured by seeing the teacher's purposeful management.
- Children who function adequately well in all areas but have a limited behaviour difficulty, for example cannot wait for their turn or share with the other children, are better placed in the mainstream class with strategies devised for their specific needs. This approach would be supported, where appropriate, by occasional visits to the nurture group for breakfast and for planned interactive activities.

The parents of children in these last three groups may be encouraged to attend parenting classes, preferably run by an outside agency but in liaison with the nurture group teacher and SENCO.

Special provision, other than the nurture group

- Children whose first language is not English, and where adequate EAL help will resolve secondary stress-related difficulties, are not appropriately placed in the nurture group. If they have *nurture* needs as well, they are offered a place, and minor EAL needs would be met in the nurturing context, as already indicated.
- Children from supportive homes who have major sensory-motor impairment, other physically based special needs or primary learning difficulties need special provision directed to their difficulties or, in the less severe cases, special educational needs support in the mainstream class from specialist teachers or TAs. Where deprivation is a major complicating factor and the difficulties are severe, a special school may be indicated.
- Children for whom a statutory assessment procedure has

already been started, or those on a statement who are waiting for a different form of provision, are placed in the nurture group only in exceptional and carefully considered circumstances, as a 'holding' operation.

- Children who appear to need long-term provision, but whose parents have refused a statutory assessment, are usually diffi-cult-to-place children for whom the nurture group can be no more than short-term expediency. Often, they are *nurture* chil-dren, with a history of major loss and change, in homes that are intrusively destructive and sometimes punitive, or are disturbed by severe mental illness, often both. It is in everyone's interests for long-term, more appropriate provision to be sought. Placing them in the group merely delays this, and reinforces the par-ents' reluctance to consider the appropriate provision. It also markedly reduces and may damage the opportunities available for the others.

These reservations are based on experience but each school has to consider the needs of the particular child, the other children and the best use of its nurture resources. The nurture group relieves stress, and is therefore a helpful resource for observation and diag-nosis in complex cases in consultation with the educational psychologist, SENCO and other relevant services.

Referral, assessment, admission and monitoring procedures

The procedures established at the beginning of the year are impor-tant in themselves; they also draw everyone into a learning experience and are the starting point for ongoing discussion.

School admission procedures

The information collected by the school prior to admission, whether from nursery, reception or Y7, and observations from induction sessions or the Common Assessment Framework (CAF) form will alert the school to any potential difficulties that the child might have in settling in. Establishing an early positive and friendly contact with parents can ease children's entry into school and give an indication of their interaction with their child and any siblings.

Initial observations are usually made in the mainstream class

Nurture group children are always on the register of a mainstream class. A period of observation under normal school conditions for at least two weeks is important. The class teachers then have a clear idea of the nature and extent of the children's difficulties and will have a more realistic appreciation of their progress in the nurture group. They will maintain a more personal contact as well as share in curriculum planning and it will be easier, when the time comes, to reintegrate them. This period of settling in is especially important for children moving from another school.

Older children

When a group is newly established, it is often the older children who are referred, for they present the most serious problems. Later, when the group is well established, it is possible to intervene earlier and admit younger children. Logically, the earlier they are referred the better, preferably as new entrants, before a pattern of resistance and cumulative failure has set in, although an older child might sometimes have a short-term need or be admitted from elsewhere.

Decision-making

Children causing anxiety are discussed by everyone involved with them. Adequate observation and discussion at this stage are the basis for regular and continuing discussion.

An established group might identify possible children in the summer term and then finalize the selection in September when usually they will be with a new teacher and possibly a new class group. Some unexpectedly settle down.

Older children who are later admissions to the school are admitted to the group only if it seems likely that they will become full members of their mainstream class at least a term before transfer to their next school. This gives them time to feel secure in their mainstream class in a familiar school environment. Whether or not they are given a place in the nurture group rests ultimately on school policy and the best use of resources. Sometimes a child is taken into the nurture group to relieve the stress on himself and on the school generally, but special thought is needed in the case of an older, markedly antisocial child who may be beyond the nurture approach.

The Boxall Profile

The Boxall Profile (Bennathan and Boxall, 1998) is the essential instrument used in nurture groups for focused teacher observations and assessment. Some schools devise their own checklists for preliminary screening (Lucas et al., 2006) before using the Boxall Profile to identify needs more precisely.

Decisions are made for positive reasons

Children are placed in the nurture group in the expectation that they are likely to make sufficient gains to be assimilated into a mainstream class within a year, or four terms at the most. The reasons are always positive and clearly formulated. Not all children can be accepted if this negates the possibility of progress for the group, though children not given a place initially might be taken in later, or visit occasionally. A policy may be needed for admitting siblings or twins. Discussion takes into account everyone's views, but as the composition of the group and the timing of admission are important, the final decision rests with the nurture teacher, SENCO and head teacher.

When the function of the nurture group is understood, children whose behaviour disturbs the class or who are unduly fearful and apprehensive, or who barely function, are usually referred quite readily. Children who are secure in the attachment they have made to their class teacher, but relate to no one else, need serious consideration as their needs are easily overlooked.

Partnership with parents and carers

The way in which parents and carers are kept informed about children's special educational needs will be set out in the school's SEN policy. They will be aware of their child's difficulties from regular discussions with the class teacher and/or SENCO and referral to the nurture group will be suggested as a possible next step if needed. In the case of new entrants, some may already be known from nursery or a children's centre or through an older sibling. The suggestion may come from social services, the local child mental health services or the health visitor. In schools that have become a focal point for the local community, and where the nurture group is known and accepted, the approach is easier. Many parents welcome an opportunity to discuss the children's difficulties and welcome the offer of a place. Most of them, sometimes after initial resistance or distress, accept the group with positive feelings. A small minority, particularly those who are not familiar with UK schools, are concerned about the informality of the surroundings and find it difficult to accept that school work is done there, and that play in the group is purposeful and educational. Occasionally, they refuse, but accept the nurture group later, after further discussion, when it is clear to them that the child's difficulties still persist. Sometimes, when psychiatric help is felt to be more appropriate and has been suggested and refused, the nurture group is accepted as the lesser of two unwelcome alternatives. Others are driven by desperation to accept the nurture group, too disturbed and fraught to understand or even care. Occasionally, there are considerable difficulties in making contact. Letters are not answered, appointments are not attended, and persistence and a great deal of pressure may be needed to get a minimal response.

Wherever possible, sympathetic discussion is usually reassuring, and a visit to the nurture group can dramatically change any negative views when they see the range of children taken into the group and realize that the teacher requires a great deal of the children and has high standards and maintains links with the other classes. Reluctance to accept a place in the nurture group arises less often when the school has a productive relationship with the parents and carers from the beginning, before major difficulties are evident, and is extremely unusual when the group is an established part of the school. The group is held in high regard and the opportunity of a place for their child is welcomed and some ask for it. If the place is refused, the child remains in the mainstream class with whatever support is possible.

Referral procedure: a summary

- Concern is expressed by member/s of staff and/or parents/carers. Normally, the class teacher voices anxiety to the SENCO initially, following the SEN Code of Practice, and this will have been recorded at School Action stage. Discussion is based on any pre-school information available, earlier recorded concerns, contact with the parents and their concerns, the class teacher's observations, assessments and any preliminary screening.
- Further observations of the child in the mainstream class are made by the nurture teacher and SENCO and, if possible, the head teacher. There is further discussion at a staff meeting. Everyone in the school is involved.
- Where appropriate, the educational psychologist makes an individual assessment, but this is not a statutory requirement and is rarely necessary.
- The class teacher completes the Boxall Profile with the nurture staff. This gives an initial assessment of the nature and extent of the child's early developmental learning needs and a starting point for intervention.
- The class teacher and the head teacher meet the parents/carers, with the child, to seek their views, and to discuss the school's concerns and a possible place in the nurture group. The observations made in school, often focusing on poor attention and progress, are discussed in relation to this. They visit the nurture group to see how it runs and to talk to the staff, and they consider how their child can be helped there.
- A decision is made by the head teacher, nurture group teacher, SENCO and class teacher in conjunction with the parents/carers.
- If it seems that the nurture group is appropriate provision, there is a general discussion in the school about the child's needs within the group, and likely progress.

- A review date is set, e.g. at half-term for a full-time group, with termly reviews to follow. The aim is to monitor adequately the child's progress to eventual integration within his mainstream class.
- Between one and four terms in the nurture group is usual when this is full-time provision. Where a longer period than this is anticipated, it is because there is good reason to believe that the child will eventually become a full member of his mainstream class.

Nurture by definition comes before nursery, and so ideally children are transferred to the group as soon as difficulties are identified. Logically, the nurture group should be an induction-to-school class for all new school entrants felt to be at risk.

Induction to the group

The procedure for admission of the children to the nurture group varies. Usually, when the group is being newly formed, the children are introduced in twos or threes over the first few days, for relatively short periods. If the group is continuing from the year before, newcomers are admitted slowly. They become familiar with the room, are introduced to simple activities and are given all the help they need to cope with these. Trust and confidence develop. As they become used to each other, their time is gradually built up. The procedure varies with the child, and with the circumstances in the nurture group and in the mainstream class.

A slow induction is particularly helpful for children who are markedly inexperienced and unventuring, or are functioning at a very early level. They are usually biddable in this restricted situation and with reassurance readily make an attachment, and quickly become familiar with the layout of the room, the adults and their expectations and the resources put out for them. They also become familiar with the basic routine and other requirements are made clear at this stage, for example 'no fighting'. During this introductory period, the children have the concentrated attention of an adult and are introduced to activities that are developmentally appropriate, enjoyable and satisfying. They are therefore likely, far more than in the mainstream class, to give concentrated attention to the adult and to their activities.

A group of 12 children is usually established over a period of two or three weeks. Children continuing from the previous year are likely to be well settled and can be reassured by the admission of new children.

Managing late entrants to the group

Difficulties can arise when there are latecomers to a group that has settled and is functioning well. Often, they react with worsening behaviour or become inhibited and immobilized. Fortunately, the other children seem to expect that the newcomers will get extra attention. Clearly, the most difficult situation of all is created by the arrival of a new entrant to a group that is still unstable.

Special efforts are needed to settle the newcomers in. It can be useful and appropriate to take all the children through the early basic organization and routines again, as this reinforces the process for those with more experience. At any one time, there are some children who will need immediate support and help, others will be able to do more on their own, while one or two will be almost ready to move on to their mainstream class.

Planning, monitoring and recording progress

Schools generally require the nurture group staff to follow the agreed curriculum planning and assessment format and process. Information from the Boxall Profile contributes to the targets for the nurture group children (see Chapters 3, 4 and 5). Broadly, the process is as follows:

- The nurture teacher has frequent discussions about the children with the class teacher and with teachers with special areas of responsibility where their expertise is needed (EAL, speech and language development, etc.).
- Meetings are arranged more formally with the head teacher, class teacher and SENCO, usually at the end of each half-term, to review the progress of all the children in the group. If other agencies are involved, a date is arranged for an inclusive review. Depending on the child's special needs, this might include the

speech therapist, occupational therapist, education welfare officer (EWO) or school nurse, and sometimes a psychiatric social
worker or psychiatrist is involved. A contribution from social
services is sought and, wherever possible, agreed lines of communication are established.

• Daily notes are kept of curriculum work, social relationships,
participation in shared activities and children's self-chosen
activities. A specially devised Weekly Record Form is recommended (Lucas et al., 2006).

• The Boxall Profile will have been completed before admission to
the group and the nurture practitioners usually repeat this after
three weeks or so to provide a baseline for their progress in the
group.

• Initial assessment otherwise follows the overall procedures of
the school. It is usual to keep samples of the child's work and
reading levels.

• Thereafter, the teacher keeps an ongoing descriptive account of
progress and the Weekly Record Form on a nurture-level child,
and completes a Boxall Profile, termly. A record is made of any
changed or particularly stressful circumstances and a note of
any contact with the parents or carers.

• At the end of each term, and always on leaving the group, a
final description of the child and the progress made is recorded,
and a Boxall Profile is completed. This is in addition to curriculum records required by the school.

• Towards the end of each term, the nurture teacher invites the
parents and carers to talk more formally about their child's
progress, though many will have been regular visitors to the
group and will be well informed already. A record is kept of the
discussion.

• A major review takes place at the end of the year, or end of the
spring term if children are in Y2 or Y6. If necessary, and in full
consultation with the parents/carers and staff, a child is referred
to the educational psychologist for assessment. In most cases,
however, the Boxall Profile together with assessment of their
curriculum work, general progress and interests will indicate
that they are ready to begin reintegration. Wherever possible,
this is discussed with the parents/carers two or three weeks
before the process begins.

Return to the mainstream class

Children have had contact with their mainstream class from the beginning and their progress is known to the class teacher through ongoing discussion and regular contact. S/he knows that eventually they will return to the class full-time. S/he also knows that the nurture teacher will continue to have a responsibility for discussion and support, and will usually monitor progress for at least a year.

The process of return to the mainstream class – the time of day, the work that will be done there – is negotiated with the class teacher. It varies from child to child but is always discussed and carefully planned.

Managing the transition

When several children in the nurture group are from the same class, the children are re-settled in ones and twos. The stability of the receiving class is important and it provides an example of more mature behaviour.

Transition is a delicate process and requires a sympathetic acceptance of the children by the receiving teacher and an interest in understanding their needs in detail. The aim of all the adults is to help the children develop the necessary personal resources for successful participation in the mainstream class. While they have made progress in the nurture group and have adequate continuing support from the nurture staff during this critical period, they also need adequate and continuing coordinated support planned in conjunction with the receiving class teacher, and carefully controlled contact with this class.

The first lessons chosen for the reintegrating child to share with the class are usually those that are most structured, such as music or PE. The strategies are planned in the context of a sympathetic shared understanding of the child's difficulties and needs. It presupposes that the receiving class teachers are positive and constructive in their attitude to the nurture group.

For all but the most undeveloped and poorly organized children, contact with their mainstream class is gradually increased as they become increasingly able to cope. The classic nurture group is not a separate unit within the school – it is an integral part of it, and easy contact is therefore possible. The class teacher has a continuing responsibility for the children and their progress is a matter for shared celebration.

Where a nurture group is a central resource serving a group of schools, it will be especially important to plan for links with the base school to be maintained in readiness for reintegration. An aspect of this process which is often overlooked is the cost; finance must be made available to support a programme for adults to be able to visit and accompany a child travelling during school hours between schools.

Whatever the organization of the school, and the nature of the contacts that are made, it is important that the nurture teacher is a familiar person about the school or group of schools and that there is recognition of her/his continuing effort to work with a considerable number of other adults. Crucial to the long-term positive outcome for the children is maintaining the interest and goodwill of all involved until the children are fully part of their mainstream class.

Indicators for return to the mainstream class

The class teacher and nurture staff sense that the time has come for disengaging the children from the nurture group and this will be borne out by the improvement in scores on the Developmental Strands of the Boxall Profile. Eagerness to be part of the mainstream class and an improvement in National Curriculum assessments are also a good indication that they are ready to move on.

Although some of the children make the transition from the nurture group with very little direct help, and may take the initiative to go, the loosening of ties is more difficult for others, and the step forward into the mainstream class is a very big one. It is as big as the normally developing younger child takes when going to school for the first time. It is indeed bigger, because the security the nurture child gets from the nurture staff is against a background of insecurity, and so leaving the nurture group may be particularly difficult.

Providing support

A child in the nurture group who is venturing into the mainstream class needs the same kind of help that supportive parents intuitively provide when their children first go to school. They will already be familiar with the inside of the classroom and will have an expectation that enjoyable things happen there. They know the teacher and that s/he is expecting them. The nurture teacher and class teacher choose the time of day when the mainstream class is most settled, and a class activity that is familiar and where sufficient support will be possible. They may take with them work prepared by the nurture teacher, something that has been accomplished successfully in the nurture group and enjoyed. At first, this is a structured task that requires little initiative, and can be completed quickly and successfully. The class teacher is alert to acknowledge their effort and success, or to provide help in good time if they appear to be struggling. Some children may not have the competence to persist with a task on their own, but can manage storytime. Each child needs individual consideration, and a successful outcome depends on the close liaison of nurture teacher and class teacher. When the children have completed the task, or have had enough, they are taken back. They tell the nurture teacher what they have done and show their work. The class teacher makes it clear that s/he wants them to come again soon. If the situation goes wrong, positive comments are still important and it might be suggested that they try again tomorrow; the situation is reviewed and modified, and extra supports are built in.

The time is increased gradually from up to one hour, or even one half-day, to perhaps two or three times a week. The situation becomes more complex and fluid, and requires more competence, confidence and self-control. If they seem to be coping, and at registration time the teacher senses that they seem settled, they stay for a full day and eventually full-time. They can return to the nurture group for visits at times of stress if it seems needed, or by arrangement at the end of the day. Knowing that the nurture staff are still there for them relieves any stress. At this stage, they are no longer visitors to the mainstream class; they are full members of the class, and are the responsibility of the class teacher.

These planned ventures into the mainstream class are usually successful because of the efforts of all involved. Just occasionally, a situation might be misjudged and there are difficulties if the school community generally is unstable, but many of the children manage to maintain a satisfactory and even high standard of behaviour in their mainstream class. The extra effort they have to make is sometimes released in restless, excited and immature behaviour when they return to the nurture group, but the advantages are felt to outweigh the possibility of a humiliating tantrum in front of the other children.

'Letting go'

It is important that 'letting go' is not too long delayed. The children need the experience of being with others who are more mature than they are, and there seems to be a critical point when they are able to respond to the expectations of their mainstream class and make better progress there, even though their problems are not fully resolved. This is a matter of fine judgement and entails risk. The children for the most part enjoy these ventures into their mainstream class and often seem able to maintain a higher level of behaviour there than in the nurture group, and their concern to behave well suggests that they experience this as an achievement. This is very much like the achievement of normally developing children when they go to school: they function at a relatively high level in school but may be immature and babyish when they return home. Some children, however, need the special sheltering of the nurture group for a longer time, and any visit to their mainstream class, however brief, would be counterproductive. They may protest that they want to go, not knowing what is going on there but wanting it all the same. Their pleas are resisted and they are easily diverted with a special activity.

Some of the children have built up a very close relationship with the nurture staff, and particularly like going back to the nurture group to visit, though they very soon begin to refer to the mainstream class teacher as 'my real teacher'. The tie with the nurture group is maintained for as long as the children need it, but is gradually loosened as they become less dependent on immediate support and reassurance. Some KS1 children look in on the nurture group after they have transferred to KS2, and some secondary school children and children who have left school have called in on a primary group for a friendly chat, or when in trouble, and have sent Christmas cards. These long-term contacts are of a mature order. The children look around the class, notice changes, recall events and like to exchange news. It is tremendously rewarding for the nurture staff to see the children again and to know that they are making good progress.

During the transitional phase, for some time they seem very close to the nurture staff at one moment and very dependent, and then suddenly are very independent. Staff sometimes feel rejected and a group of them expressed this ruefully at a meeting. Most of them were mothers and they commented with considerable feeling about themselves as mothers in relation to their own children: 'Teacher is everything in the world for six-year-olds. They don't stop to kiss you goodbye when they are going to school, don't even look over their shoulder.'

Evaluation

Providing evidence of the work of the nurture group is a vital part of school evaluation and improvement and should be included on the School Evaluation Form (SEF) in readiness for the Ofsted inspection. Some LAs have systems for collecting data from nurture groups for evaluation purposes and the nurture staff will be responsible for providing this.

Additional information about the work of the nurture group, including qualitative data in the form of case studies, especially where there is long-term contact with a family and samples of the children's work, can be very powerful in demonstrating the benefits of the group to both the individual children and to the school community as a whole, and may have long-term value for nurture groups into the future.

Summary ☐

- The children's successful return to the mainstream class is the desired outcome; the process is agreed and involves all staff in working together.

- Reflective observation and assessment are ongoing and essential for the school's formal procedures to be effective.

- Admission to the nurture group is for positive reasons; parents are kept fully informed and other agencies are involved as required. Nurture group provision is not appropriate for every child.

- Evidence of the nurture group's work is important, both for the school and for the future of nurture groups.

Further reading

Frost, N. and Parton, N. (2009) *Understanding Social Care: Politics, Policy and Practice*. London: Sage Publications. Interagency collaboration in children's services is a work in progress and this book provides an up-to-date picture.

Webster-Stratton, C. (1999) *How to Promote Children's Social and Emotional Competence*. London: Paul Chapman Publishing. This text will be familiar to other professionals and could be a useful resource.

Children whose difficulties are attributed to ASD or ADHD are increasingly being referred to nurture groups and there is a growing amount of literature available. The respective websites www.teacch.com and www.addiss.co.uk are a useful first point of contact.

Bibliography

Ainsworth, M.D.S. (1978) *Patterns of Attachment: A Psychological Study of the Strange Situation*. London: Wiley.

Altrichter, H., Feldman, A., Posch, P. and Somekh, B. (2008) *Teachers Investigate their Work: An Introduction to Action Research Across the Professions*. London: Routledge.

Axup, T. and Gersch, I. (2008) 'The impact of challenging student behaviour upon teachers' lives in a secondary school: teachers' perceptions', *British Journal of Special Education* 35(3): 144–51.

Batmanghelidjh, C. (2006) *Shattered Lives: Children who Live with Courage and Dignity*. London: Jessica Kingsley.

Bennathan, M. and Boxall, M. (1996) *Effective Intervention in Primary Schools: Nurture Groups*. London: David Fulton.

Bennathan, M. and Boxall, M. (1998) *The Boxall Profile Handbook: A Guide to Effective Intervention in the Education of Pupils with Social, Emotional and Behavioural Difficulties*. London: Nurture Group Network.

Bennathan, M. and Boxall, M. (2000) *Effective Intervention in Primary Schools. Nurture Groups*. London: David Fulton Publishers.

Bennathan, M. and Rose, J. (2008) *All About Nurture Groups*. London: Nurture Group Network.

Benner, G.J., Nelson, J.R. and Epstein, M.H. (2002) 'Summary of language skills of children with EBD: a literature review', *Journal of Emotional and Behavioural Disorders*. Available at: www.literacytrust.org.uk [accessed 10 July 2009].

Bishop, S. (2008) *Running a Nurture Group*. London: Paul Chapman Publishing.

Bomber, L.M. (2007) *Inside I'm Hurting: Practical Strategies for Supporting Children with Attachment Difficulties in Schools*. London: Worth Publishing.

Bottery, M. (2004) *The Challenge of Educational Leadership: Values in a Globalized Age*. London: Paul Chapman Publishing.

Bowlby, J. (1953) *Child Care and the Growth of Love*. Harmondsworth: Penguin.

Bowlby, J. (1969) *Attachment and Loss, Vol. 1: Attachment.* London: Hogarth Press.

Boxall, M., Holmes, E. and Lucas, S. (2000) 'Learning and the Brain', *AWCEBD National Newsletter.* Summer.

Bruce, T. (1996) *Helping Young Children to Play.* London: Hodder and Stoughton.

Bruce, T. (1997) *Early Childhood Education,* 2nd edition. London: Hodder and Stoughton.

Bruner, J. (1960) *The Process of Education.* Cambridge, MA: Harvard University Press.

Caul, L. (2003) *Dealing with Violent Behaviour in Schools.* NSIN Research Matters. Institute of Education, University of London.

CCETSW (1978) *Good Enough Parenting: Report of a Group on Work with Children and Young People and the Implications for Social Work Education.* London: CCETSW.

Claxton, G. (2000) 'The anatomy of intuition', in T. Atkinson and G. Claxton (eds) *The Intuitive Practitioner: On the Value of not Always Knowing what One is Doing.* Maidenhead: Open University Press.

Claxton, G. (2002) *Building Learning Power: Helping Young People Become Better Learners.* Bristol: TLO.

Cline, T. (2006) 'Foreword', in S. Lucas, K. Insley and G. Buckland (2006) *Nurture Group Principles and Curriculum Guidelines: Helping Children to Achieve.* London: Nurture Group Network.

Cooper, P. (2001). *We Can Work it Out: What Works in Educating Children with Social, Emotional and Behavioural Difficulties Outside Mainstream Classrooms?* Ilford: Barnardos.

Cooper, P. (2002) 'The Nurture Group Research Project', *AWCEBD Newsletter,* Summer. http//www.nurturegroups.org/data/files/downloads/nurture_groups.doc.

Cooper, P. and Whitebread, D. (2007) 'The effectiveness of nurture groups on student progress: evidence from a national research study', *Emotional and Behavioural Difficulties* 12(3): 171–90.

Crittenden, P.M. (1992) 'Treatment of anxious attachment in infancy and early childhood'. *Development and Psychopathology,* 4: 575–602. Cambridge University Press USA.

Daniels, A. and Williams, H. (2000) 'Reducing the need for exclusions and statements for behaviour: The Framework for intervention (Part 1)', *Educational Psychology in Practice* 15(4): 220–7.

DCSF (2007a) *Guidance on the Duty to Promote Community Cohesion.* Available at: www.nationalstrategies.gov.uk [accessed 22 Sept 2009].

DCSF(2007b) *The Children's Plan – Building Brighter Futures.* London: The Stationery Office.

DCSF (2007c) *The Use of Force to Control or Restrain Pupils.* London: The Stationery Office.

DCSF (2008a) *Early Years Foundation Stage.* London: The Stationery Office.

DCSF (2008b) *Every Child a Talker: Guidance for Early Language Lead Practitioners.* Available at: www.nationalstrategies.gov.uk [accessed 22 Sept 2009].

DCSF (2008c) *The Bercow Review: A Review of Services for Children and Young People (0–19) with Speech, Language and Communication Needs.* London: The Stationery Office.

DCSF (2009a) *Learning Behaviour: Lessons Learned.* London: The Stationery Office.

DCSF (2009b) *Your Child, Your Schools, Our Future: Building a 21st Century School System.* London: The Stationery Office.

DCSF (2009c) *The Lamb Inquiry: Special Educational Needs and Parental Confidence; Inspection, Accountability and School Improvement.* London: The Stationery Office.

DCSF (2009d) *Gaining Ground Initiative.* London: The Stationery Office.

DES (1989) *Discipline in Schools, Report of the Committee of Enquiry, Chaired by Lord Elton.* London: HMSO.

DfEE (1998) *The National Literacy Strategy: Framework for Teaching.* London: DfEE Publications.

DfEE/QCA (1999) *The National Curriculum.* Norwich: HMSO.

DfES (2001a) *Inclusive Schooling.* London: DfES.

DfES (2001b) *Special Educational Needs: Code of Practice.* London: DfES.

DfES (2001c) *Supporting School Improvement: Emotional and Behavioural Development.* London: QCA.

DfES (2003a) *Every Child Matters.* London: DfES.

DfES (2003b) *Raising Standards and Tackling Workload: A National Agreement.* Available at: www.tda.gov.uk [accessed 20 November 2009].

DfES (2005) *Children's Workforce Strategy: A Strategy to Build a*

World-class Workforce for Children and Young People. London: HMSO.

Duffy, B. (1998) *Supporting Creativity and Imagination in the Early Years*. Buckingham and Philadelphia, PA: Open University Press.

Fineman, S. (ed.) (2000) *Emotion in Organizations*. London: Sage Publications.

Frederickson, N. and Cline, T. (2002) *Special Educational Needs, Inclusion and Diversity: A Textbook*. Buckingham: Open University Press.

Frost, N. and Parton, N. (2009) *Understanding Children's Social Care: Politics, Policy and Practice*. London: Sage Publications.

Furlong, J. (2000) 'Intuition and the crisis in teacher professionalism', in T. Atkinson and G. Claxton (eds) *The Intuitive Practitioner: On the Value of not Always Knowing what One is Doing*. Maidenhead: Open University Press.

Geddes, H. (2006) *Attachment in the Classroom: The Links between Children's Early Experience, Emotional Well-being and Performance in School*. London: Worth Publishing.

Gerhardt, S. (2004) *Why Love Matters: How Affection Shapes a Baby's Brain*. Hove and New York: Brunner-Routledge.

Goldschmied, E. (1987) *Babies at Work* (video). London: National Children's Bureau.

Goldschmied, E. and Jackson, S. (2004) *People Under Three – Young Children in Day Care*. London: Routledge.

Gopnik, A. (2009) *The Philosophical Baby: What Children's Minds Tell Us about Truth, Love and the Meaning of Life*. London: Bodley Head.

Gopnik, A., Metzoff, A.N. and Kuhl, P.K. (1999) *How Babies Think*. London: Weidenfeld and Nicholson.

Greeley, K. (2000) *Why Fly that Way? Linking Community and Academic Achievement*. New York: Teachers College Press.

Greenfield, S. (1999) Learning and the Brain: A Public Enquiry. The Lifelong Learning Foundation and the Royal Institution Seminar, Royal Institution, London, 23 October.

Greenfield, S. (2001) *The Private Life of the Brain*. London: Penguin Books.

Grossman, K., Grossman, K.E. and Kindler, H. (2005) 'Early care and the roots of attachment and partnership representations: the Bielefeld and Regensburg longitudinal studies', in K.E.

Grossman, K. Grossman and E. Waters (eds) *Attachment from Infancy to Adulthood: The Major Longitudinal Studies*. New York: Guilford.

Howes, A., Emanuel, J. and Farrell, P. (2002) 'Can nurture groups facilitate inclusive practice in primary schools?', in P. Farrell and M. Ainscow (eds) *Making Special Education Inclusive: From Research to Practice*. London: David Fulton Publishers.

Insley, K. and Lucas, S. (2009) 'Making the most of the relationship between two adults to impact on early childhood pedagogy: raising standards and narrowing the attainment gap', in T. Papatheodorou and J. Moyles (eds) *Learning Together in the Early Years*. London: Routledge.

James, A. and James, A. (2008) *Key Concepts in Childhood Studies*. London: Sage Publications.

Jones, E., Homes, R. and Powell, J. (eds) (2005) *Early Childhood Studies: A Multi-professional Perspective*. Buckingham: Open University Press.

Katz, L.G. (2002) 'A developmental approach to the curriculum in the early years', in A. Pollard (ed.) *Readings for Reflective Teaching*. London: Continuum.

Keenan, T. and Evans, S. (2009) *An Introduction to Child Development*. London: Sage Publications.

Kounin, J. (1970) 'Discipline and group management in classrooms', in A. Pollard (ed.) (2002) *Readings for Reflective Teaching*. London: Continuum.

Laird, G. (2009) 'Babies help boys reach new maturity', *Times Educational Supplement* 20, February. [Accessed 9 June 2009]

Layard, R. and Dunn, J. (2009) *A Good Childhood – Searching for Values in a Competitive Age*. London: Children's Society.

Lewin, R. and Birute, R. (2000) *Weaving Complexity and Business: Engaging the Soul at Work*. New York: TEXERE LLC.

Lindsay, G. and Peacey, N. (2009) *Lamb Inquiry: Local Authorities' Learning from the Eight Projects*. Available at www.dcsf.gov.uk [accessed 20 November 2009]

Loughran, J., Mitchell, I. and Mitchell, J. (eds) (2002) *Learning from Teacher Research*. Sydney: Allen and Unwin.

Lucas, D. (2003) *Halibut Jackson*. London: Andersen Press.

Lucas, S. (1999) 'The nurturing school: the impact of nurture group principles and practice on the whole school', *Emotional and Behavioural Difficulties* 4(3): 14–19.

Lucas, S., Insley, K. and Buckland, G. (2006) *Nurture Group Principles and Curriculum Guidelines: Helping Children to Achieve.* London: Nurture Group Network.

Maynard, T. (2007) 'Forest Schools in Great Britain: an initial exploration', *Contemporary Issues in Early Childhood* 8(4): 320–31.

McNeil, F.(1999) *Brain Research and Learning: An Introduction.* NSIN Research Matters. Institute of Education, University of London.

McNeil, F. (2008) *Learning with the Brain in Mind.* London: Sage Publications.

Mosley, J. (1996) *Quality Circle Time.* Wisbech: LDA.

Murray, L. and Andrews, L. (2005) *The Social Baby: Understanding Babies' Communication from Birth.* London: CP Publishing.

O'Brien, L. (2009) 'Learning outdoors: the Forest School approach', *Education 3–13* 37(1): 45–60.

Ofsted (1997) *The Annual Report of Her Majesty's Chief Inspector of Schools: Standards and Quality in Education 1995/96.* London: HMSO.

Ofsted (2005) *Managing Challenging Behaviour.* London: HMI. Available at: www.ofsted.gov.uk [accessed 7 July 2009]

Pagliano, P. (2000) *Multisensory Environments.* London: David Fulton Publishers.

Pollard, A. (ed.) (2002) *Readings for Reflective Teaching.* London: Continuum.

QCA (Qualifications and Curriculum Authority) (1999) *Early Learning Goals.* London: QCA.

Reed, J. and Warner-Rogers, J. (eds) (2008) *Child Neuropsychology: Concepts, Theory and Practice.* Chichester: Blackwell.

Roberts, A. (2002) *Little Book of Treasure Baskets.* London: Featherstone Education Ltd.

Robinson, M. (2003) *From Birth to One: The Year of Opportunity.* Buckingham: Open University Press.

Rose, J. (2009) *Independent Review of the Primary Curriculum: Final Report.* London: DCSF.

Rutter, M. (and the English and Romanian Adoptees Study Team) (1998) 'Developmental catch-up and deficit, following adoption after severe global privation', *Journal of Child Psychology and Psychiatry* 39(4): 465–76.

Rutter, M., Giller, H. and Hagell, A. (1998) *Antisocial Behaviour by*

Young People. Cambridge: Cambridge University Press.

Schore, A. (2003) *Affect Dysregulation and Disorders of the Self.* New York: Norton. Available at: www.thinkbody.co.uk [accessed 22 September 2009]

Social Exclusion Task Force (2007) *Reaching out: Think Family. Analysis and themes from the Families at Risk Review.* London: Cabinet Office. Available at: www.cabinetoffice.gov.uk/media/cabinetoffice/social_exclusion_task_force/assets/think_families/think_families.pdf [accessed 22 September 2009]

Somekh, B. (2006) *Action Research.* Maidenhead: Open University Press.

Sonnet, H. (2008) *Nurturing Success: How to Create and Run an Effective Nurture Group.* Wisbech: LDA.

Steer, A. (2009) *Learning Behaviour: Lessons Learned – A review of behaviour standards and practices in our schools.* London: DCSF. Available at: www.teachernet.gov.uk/publications [accessed 22 September 2009]

TDA (Training and Development Agency) (2008) *Remodelling: The National Agreement.* Available at: www.tda.gov.uk [accessed 22 September 2009]

Teicher, M.H., Andersen, S.L., Polcari, A., Anderson, C.M., Navalta, C.P. and Kim, D.M. (2003) 'The neurobiological consequences of early stress and maltreatment', in *Neuroscience and Biobehavioural Reviews* 27(1-2): 33–44.

Trevarthen, C. (1977) 'A descriptive analysis of infant communicative behaviour', in H.R. Schaffer (ed.) *Studies in Mother–Child Interaction.* New York: Academic Press.

Webster-Stratton, C. (1999) *How to Promote Children's Social and Emotional Competence.* London: Paul Chapman Publishing.

Winnicott, D.W. (1960) 'The theory of the parent infant relationship', in *The Maturational Process and the Facilitating Environment.* London: Hogarth Press.

Winnicott, D.W. (1964) *The Child, the Family and the Outside World.* Harmondsworth: Penguin.

Winnicott, D.W. (1971) *Playing and Reality.* London: Routledge.

Wood, C. and Caulier-Grice, J. (2006) *Fade or Flourish: How Primary Schools can Build on Children's Early Progress.* London: Social Market Foundation.

Index

233